Arabian Flavours

Arabian Flavours
Recipes and tales of Arab life

Salah Jamal

translated from the Spanish by Elfreda Powell

Souvenir Press

To my family
A Um Kulthum

*Within man's will is a yearning
to transform his inner cloud into a sun.*

Khalil Gibran

Fragment of A. Cresques' 'Mappamundi' (1375)

Contents

Preface to the Spanish Edition

Salah Jamal, a dermatologist by profession and a historian, is a Palestinian who has lived in Barcelona for many years. As a cultured and refined host, his aim is to make us take a hard look at our centuries-old ignorance of ethnic groups other than our own. But rather than subject us to a learned dissertation in order to enlighten our ignorance – we 'who belittle whatever we have no knowledge of' – he has chosen the braver method of dialogue, using as a starting point our daily preoccupation with our need to eat and drink. *Arabian Flavours* is much more than an Arab cookery book, but nonetheless that is what it is, and it offers specific answers to anyone who would seriously like to prepare the culinary delights of one of the world's most populous civilisations.

The first paradox of this book is that it is written by a man, and that the secrets of Arab cooking have, for centuries, been female secrets. Work in the Arab kitchen has always been woman's lot, and down through the generations, women have transmitted from one to another all there is to learn about this daily alchemy of the stove. When Salah Jamal began his research, they would say to him: 'Tell your mother not to forget such and such a spice…'or 'Tell her to put such and such into soak', for few among his informants believed that he, a man, could really be interested in practical cookery.

His book shows us very clearly just how central to our culture cooking is. It is influenced by taste, knowledge, technical skills, religious teachings, climate, life style, access to basic products, and the infiltration of influences from civilisations that are sometimes exotic and remote. The author shows us how a well-made dish contains all the characteristics of a poem, for it is a mixture of emotion, dignity, aroma, the capacity to excite, and an invitation to live more passionately. Because – within healthy limits – we cook out of love, and for love, and always with the intention of making eating pleasurable, *Arabian Flavours* quite rightly takes a hedonistic view of the art of good eating and good drinking.

This book is also a chronicle of our time, and the makings of a novel: Salah Jamal recollects for us moments of everyday life in a family of ten brothers and sisters, of childhood and adolescence, of his life's continuing journey, and the individual and collective fortunes of his people – which he wisely narrates without resorting to either epic or, even less, tragic detail. This book reminds lay readers, among whom I count myself, of the plurality and diversity of the Arab world and of the huge variety of situations that this world represents. For example, when the book mentions the ancient practice of drinking coffee or tea, fragments of global history are being pieced together along with regions that are both complementary and contrasting.

This is a book rich in irony, nostalgia and philosophical reflection: the author is fascinated by primitive methods, ovens that guarantee their own original flavours or the subtle nuance of a crunchy texture. He remembers what it is like to be hungry – hungry for many, many things. And he is scathingly funny about people who air their questionable knowledge. He talks to us about the Koran and of the Prophet's advice, about the authoritarian rigour of some Arab men and about the unspoken pleasure of occasionally eating with your hands. He tells us about lawful produce, and social rules that uphold the relationship between who answers an invitation and who invites... And he ends with a beautiful hymn to water, a product that only those who know it is as a scarce resource value and savour.

In sum, *Arabian Flavours* is much more than a treatise on Arab cooking: it's the work of an expert anthropologist.

Ignasi Riera
Cornellà de Llobregat, Barcelona, September 1999

INTRODUCTION

I remember when I first arrived in Barcelona. I had only just got to my Palestinian friends' flat, just a few hours after they'd collected me from the docks, after my long journey from Palestine via Beirut, when a strapping young man of about twenty – though he seemed older – came up to me. He was plump and unkempt, and held a glass of wine in his hand. Seeing my look of surprise, he eyed me at great length from head to toe and back again. Then he let out a long, homesick sigh and began to recite a famous Arab poem, which he had wittily tweaked:

The original verse went:

Would that my youth might return, so   الآ ليت الشباب يعود يوماً
That I could recount it my woes of old age. لا خبره بما فعل بي المشيب

And he'd changed it to the following, no less splendid, nostalgic lament:

Would that falafel *might return, so that I*   الآ ليت الفلافل يعود يوماً
Could recount it my woes from chorizo. لا خبره بما فعل بي الشوريثو

My hosts' peals of laughter astonished me. And at this point I began my own simple interpretation: in my mind the smell of *falafel*, that smell of oil which has been used for frying over and over again, came flooding back to me, for it is in this oil that those traditional, often eaten vegetable croquettes are fried in the Middle East.

The truth of it was that I was shocked to see these people caught up in this absurd, homesick talk of food. If Palestinian *falafel* were the best, where would you have them?... Was Lebanese *hommos* the best? ...Or was *maqlouba* better in this region or that?...Not one of them asked me about the civil war raging between Jordan and Palestine which at that very moment (September 1970) had reached crisis point.

Barely a few months later, I confess, I had recited the *falafel/chorizo* version hundreds of times. All the Arab students recited it too, like the Lord's Prayer, particularly in the student restaurant (where a meal cost 18 pesetas) while we got through our plates of endives and the toughest beefsteak I've ever eaten.

On many occasions in the early 1970s I set out to create an authentic Arab meal and ended with a complete failure. There were many reasons for this: not one of us had a clue about cooking; another reason was that in Spain we lacked the essential ingredients that distinguish one country's cooking from another. For example, we lacked the spices, for although they all existed, we did not know how to mix them properly to make the special one called *fulful bhar* (see p.206). We lacked the authentic small delicate aubergines, the baby courgettes, *mulukhiah*, *bamia* (okra), clarified butter, real virgin olive oil with its true Arab aroma. Added to all these difficulties were Arab students' lack of money and the expense of importing any of these products, and on top of everything else there were no grocery stores selling this type of merchandise. So, making a true Arab meal at this time was just a fantasy. I well remember the infinite number of inventions we made to make up for some of the essential ingredients that didn't exist in Spain. One fundamental dilemma was how to find a substitute for the omnipresent *tahina* (sesame paste), a basic ingredient for many traditional dishes (especially *hommos*). Curiously enough, the product we chose was yogurt. The first few times we used yogurt in *hommos* invited a good deal of derision, but as the saying goes when there's no bread, 'Let them eat cake'.

The recipes or, more accurately, the inventions were circulated among the Arab students by word of mouth, in true Middle Eastern fashion, for where I had grown up at least, books or literature on cooking methods were in short supply. And even had they existed, who would have bought them? It had always worked perfectly well with the women passing on their knowledge of the art of cooking to their daughters by word of mouth, so that they would be able to carry out their duties as a wife properly.

I can't remember where and when we prepared this 'semi-Arab food'. In fact, this was an additional difficulty, which on a few occasions was miraculously overcome. Almost all of us 500 Arab students in Barcelona (there were no more than 2,000 in the whole of Spain) lodged in private houses with 'No cooking allowed', as the small ads for 'Rooms to let' would specify at the end. But occasionally landladies or the ladies of the house (they tended to be women on their own, spinsters or widows) would return to their home village or go to the sea-side. We would then make the most of their absence by cooking up some traditional fare, and the aromas released would thrill us to the core with nostalgia and memories. When we first began doing this, we lacked guile, and the strong cooking smells betrayed us. The cost was instant expulsion, or at best, hysterical rows and economic sanctions on the use of the kitchen (clearly, we were wasting gas). But as time went on we acquired more expertise, and after we'd finished cooking, we'd spray the kitchen with French perfume, followed by the whole flat, including the staircase – we knew nothing of air fresheners at the time.

Then – allelujah! – after the war of October 1973, the price of oil shot up. Many Arabs got rich and as a consequence became increasingly extravagant. One way to squander their easy money was tourism to Europe and the USA. 'Medical attention' was the greatest excuse for this. And so the 'invalids' travelled with a grant from the state. These people had no wish to experiment with European cooking; they complained that the local food was tasteless and that their palates could not adapt to it.

*

The Lebanese blindman's guide who accompanied the 80-year-old Saudi prince was fed up with him complaining. He complained at breakfast, he complained at lunch and he complained at dinner. One day, after he had feasted on fresh seafood flown in specially from Galicia, the prince proclaimed from the depth of his heart that he would gladly pay the same thousand dollars 'for some *hommos* and fresh onion'. That nostalgic, fervent lament fired the Lebanese's enthusiastic commercial instinct.

A few months later, what was probably the first Arab restaurant in Barcelona was opened under the management of the ex blindman's guide who hadn't the faintest idea as to what was involved in preparing food. Logically, that task fell to a Palestinian, a clever and cheap worker. The restaurant was strategically located in a neighbourhood swarming with Arabs – over from the oil states – near an eye clinic which performed miracle eye surgery. It would be around this eye clinic that the first Arab restaurants would be concentrated, with mixed results.

What these pseudo 'restaurateurs' had not expected was that gradually their clientele would become mostly local, that is, from Barcelona.

Since those beginnings in Barcelona, as we know, various cities in Spain have imitated the Catalan capital's experience. Today there are Arab restaurants in almost every Spanish town. And, it has to be said, Spain was the last country in Europe to become acquainted with Arab food. Until then, the main basic products for making traditional Arab food had to be imported from Paris, Berlin, London… In spite of all this, the Spanish and especially the young Spanish are very curious and open to innovations, particularly when it comes to eating. For this reason, 'luxury' Arab restaurants have adapted to their new clientele and to its small purchasing power, and have turned themselves into bars where you can also eat. Today, in Spain, there's an abundance of snack bars cum stalls which offer the young exquisite fast food (of which the king dish is a combination of *falafel, shawermah, hommos* etc) and at very reasonable prices.

As I said earlier, the Spanish are curious and very enquiring, and they would frequently ask how one dish or other was made. The truth is that none of us knew exactly. A friend of mine never stopped asking me for 'recipes' for these dishes. Every time I was taking a trip to an Arab country, I would come back laden with traditional recipes, given me by word of mouth and only by women, who are the 'authentic' archive of Arab cooking. Women, whether they are Palestinian, Lebanese, Egyptian, Moroccan, all have something in common – that pride of possessing the key to two of the three pleasurable skills of which the Arab male frequently boasts: eating flesh (relishing their food), putting flesh into flesh (making love) and mounting flesh (riding a horse).

These women were surprised and happy to be able to talk to an Arab male interested in cookery recipes, and passed on their knowledge of local cooking with great enthusiasm, but their weather-beaten faces betrayed their utter disbelief in my ability to prepare even one simple dish. So they would carry on, interrupting one another and explaining their own experiences: 'No, no, I would put in a bit of that.' And the other would interrupt with 'Some mint leaves would be better. The other...'

I have collected hundreds of Arab recipes and ideas for cooking that would fill numerous tomes. But I asked myself whether it would be practical to compile one book of so many recipes and so many stories. Clearly, it wasn't. So I have opted for this small bouquet of aromas from the Arab world. This little book contains recipes for traditional dishes that are easy, and accessible for all abilities and all pockets. I claim 'modestly' that this way you will get to know Arab food, become familiar with it, solve its mystery, taste it and, I hope, prepare it yourself.

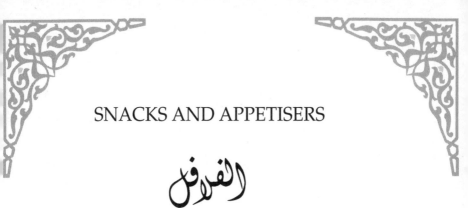

SNACKS AND APPETISERS

الفلافل

FALAFEL
Vegetable croquettes

Salvation of the poor

You may be wondering why I should begin this book with *falafel*. Well, it's an obvious choice. *Falafel* is the most popular ready-to-serve food in the Near East – including non-Arab countries too. Its name most probably derives from the Arab verb *falfala*, which means 'to season'. It's fair to say that in general *falafel* has the most varied and balanced amounts of spices of all Arab dishes. *Falafel* is eaten at any time of day, breakfast, lunch, an afternoon break, dinner, or simply as a snack. It's also eaten as an hors d'oeuvre or side dish, and for thousands of families who are not well off it will frequently be their main meal. And a sandwich of *falafel* on its own, if it's properly made and well spiced, can, in fact, be as satisfying as a full-course meal.

Falafel is ubiquitous and you will find it being sold on any city street corner in the Near East. In Egypt it goes by the name of *taameya*. In the Maghreb (the region of North Africa, that comprises the coastlands and the Atlas ranges: Algeria, Morocco and Tunisia), however, it's not so well known as in the rest of the Muslim-Arab world. In the towns every living quarter is pleasurably redolent with the smell of the oil in which *falafel* are fried, as redolent as the scent of jasmine – a flower that is equally ubiquitous in every corner of the Muslim-Arab world.

The origin of these *falafel* croquettes has been debated a great deal, but in all probability they were being eaten in Egypt at the time of the Pharaohs, and from there they spread to the Arabian peninsula, especially to the Yemen. At the beginning of the twentieth century, when oil was discovered, wave upon wave of people migrated from the Near East to the oil regions. Thousands of Yemeni families emigrated north to Saudi Arabia and Kuwait in search of a better life. There they met up with other emigrants who came from the north – Palestinians, Syrians etc. – and with thousands of families from North Africa. On many street corners in these flourishing areas, the Yemeni set up their little market stalls for *falafel*. This cheap, fast food rapidly became all the rage among the emigrant workers' gang leaders, for these workers made up 70 per cent of the population of the Arabian Gulf. Years later, many of them returned to their native countries with a small fortune, and set up a host of outlets for selling *falafel*. So, consequently, the Syrians, the Palestinians, the Lebanese, the Iraqis and even the Israelis all claim *falafel* as their own national dish.

FALAFEL
Vegetable croquettes

Serves 6-8

Ingredients

250 grams (9 oz) dried broad beans
250 grams (9 oz) dried chickpeas
2-3 medium garlic cloves

5 medium onions
½ cup freshly chopped parsley
½ cup freshly chopped coriander
2 teaspoons salt
2 tablespoons plain flour
½ teaspoon hot red pepper, such as Cayenne
½ teaspoon bicarbonate of soda
½ teaspoon black pepper
½ teaspoon cumin
½ teaspoon ground cinnamon
3 dessertspoons baking powder
6 cups (see page 206 for imperial and metric equivalents) vegetable oil
for frying the falafel croquettes
2 cups water

Method

- Put the broad beans and chickpeas to soak for 12 hours or overnight.
- Peel and chop the onions and garlic. Mix with the parsley and coriander.
- Add the chickpeas and beans to the mixture and pass them all through a mincer so that you end up with a lumpy mass.
- Add the spices, herbs, salt, bicarbonate of soda, flour, baking powder, water, hot red pepper (cayenne). Knead them together.
- Allow the mixture to rest for 1-1½ hours.
- Using your fingers or a spoon, shape the mixture into small round or oblong croquettes, taking care not to make them too bulky.
- Heat the oil to very hot in a deep frying pan or fryer, then add the croquettes and fry them till golden brown. Then take them out.

SUGGESTIONS

In the Arab world there is a cooking utensil for shaping *falafel*. You can sometimes find it in shops that sell Middle Eastern products.

The croquettes can be eaten whatever way you like, although the most traditional way is to put them inside some Arab bread with some thin slices of tomato, a bit of lettuce, slices of gherkin, onion, *tahina* and a pinch of chilli. You can also serve them on a plate, with all or part of the garnish I have just mentioned.

HOMMOS
Chickpea purée

Teachers' fix

Hommos and *falafel*, *falafel* and *hommos*... it makes no odds in which order you say them, when it comes to gastronomic excellence throughout the Middle East, these are the dominant foods. Except for the Bedouin, it is impossible to meet anyone from no matter what race or religion of the many that abound in this part of the world who does not eat *hommos* at least three or four times a week.

From when this dish began its life at the beginning of the twentieth century, up until the 1970s, it was considered uniquely a breakfast food. Its particular aroma, together with the scent of raw fresh onion, the usual accompaniment to *hommos*, is always an unmistakable reminder for me of those early morning walks between home and school when I was a small boy. We schoolboys would walk down the centre of the long narrow paved street of the Kasbah which ran right through the ancient city of Nablus. In early morning all along the street and cross-streets, small groups of shopkeepers and stallholders would cluster together – and they still do – everyone holding their plate of *hommos*, under the protection and blessing of verses from the Koran intoned by the *Sheij* Abdel Baset (the best), issuing forth from transistor radios in the shops.[1]*

*Notes begin on page 203.

Although, as a dish, it is very small and contains only a small quantity of purée, those eating it give passersby a simple glance and automatically greet them with the word *tfaduluh* (which is an invitation to eat).

This is a venerated custom in every Middle Eastern town, not only among shopkeepers, but you'll find office workers, civil servants and teachers all doing the same. I remember my dreaded masters, too, going round at breakfast time with this particular dish, an onion in their hand, relaxed and happy. The first class of the day was, without a doubt, the most agreeable of all, if we compared it with those that followed. The masters were more permissive, more through pleasurable inertia than through conscious intention. The sole reason for this was to be found in this same breakfast, repeated day after day – a combination of the chickpea purée, fresh onion and Arab bread, and, to finish off, a cup of mint or sage tea – which induced, even among the sharpest, an incurable feeling of relaxation and mental calm. The first lesson of the day was always, too, a period of transition or mental conditioning for the lessons that followed. To drive the point home, the maths lesson was always scheduled as the first in the day, to take advantage of the teacher's mental clarity as much as the pupils'. This became obvious in our exam results. I have always asked myself – and not just in jest – why there are so many good mathematicians in the Arab world, even though it was the cradle of that discipline. Could *hommos* be to blame for this phenomenon? In Egypt they say *mdammas* (broad bean purée) is the reason. The Egyptians, who claim fame for being the wittiest in the Arab world, instead of putting someone down with classic adjectives like 'empty-headed', 'mad' or 'idiotic' say 'they have their head stuffed with *mdammas*'.

Hommos, falafel and *mdammas* are relatively unknown in the Maghreb region of North Africa, and if you do come across some place that serves them, it can be put down to those Maghrebi emigrants from Europe who came into contact with Arab emigrants from the Middle East.

These dishes cost little, which is why they are very popular. Today an infinite variety of ingredients quite foreign to the original ones are added to them, though, in fact, no modern variation is better than the original preparation for this dish.

HOMMOS
Chickpea purée

Serves 2

Ingredients

250 grams (9 oz) cooked chickpeas (tinned or in a jar)
1 level teaspoon salt
2 medium cloves garlic, crushed (because of garlic's strong flavour, this quantity can be adjusted according to personal taste,
¼ cup lemon juice
¼ cup tahina
½ cup water
1 tablespoon of yogurt (optional: it is used to whiten the purée)

Method

- *Beat all the ingredients in a mixer until you have a slightly solid purée.*
- *Spread the purée on to a flat dish and decorate with some whole cooked chickpeas, little pools of olive oil, sprigs of fresh parsley and a pinch of ground cumin. If you want a finer, more uniform purée, put the chickpeas through an electric blender.*

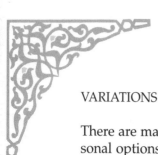

VARIATIONS

There are many variations of *hommos*, although all are personal options and owe nothing to traditional races or geographical locations; nonetheless, care is taken to present the dish in certain ways. For example, some cooks garnish the dish with slices of onion in the centre and minced meat fried in oil.

SUGGESTIONS

The most frequent problem one finds when preparing *hommos* is the final texture, after all the ingredients have been beaten together. To obtain a satisfactory texture you should observe these small details:

– If the purée's texture is too liquid, add a tablespoonful of chickpeas and another one of *tahina*, since both these ingredients will give it a more solid consistency.
– If the texture is too 'doughy', gradually add small quantities of water to obtain the desired texture.

MDAMMAS
Broad bean purée

Everything I have explained about *hommos* also applies to *mdammas*. Although the broad bean plant is a native of Persia, *mdammas* is a dish that originated in Egypt and the Sudan, and is undoubtedly the most popular food in these countries.

Nonetheless, and according to my modest culinary criteria, neither the Egyptians nor the Sudanese, but rather the Arabs of Asia Minor (the Palestinians, Jordanians, Syrians, Lebanese and Iraqis) are the true masters when it comes to preparing the most delicious version of this dish.

MDAMMAS
Broad bean purée (Egyptian and Sudanese version)

Serves 2

Ingredients

250 grams (9 oz) cooked purple broad beans (tin or jar)
1 teaspoon salt
1 tablespoon olive oil
1 raw tomato, chopped
1 pinch hot red pepper (Cayenne)
1 red or green pepper cut into tiny pieces
1 onion chopped very finely

29

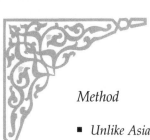

Method

- Unlike Asian Arabs, the Egyptians and Sudanese boil the beans for a long time, so there is no need to mash them up. Drain them and put them on a dish.
- Cover them with the rest of the ingredients and serve the mdammas accompanied by eish *(meaning life): Arab bread.*

ASIA MINOR VERSION OF MDAMMAS

Serves 2

Ingredients

250 grams (9 oz) cooked purple broad beans (tin or jar)
1 large clove of garlic
1 teaspoon salt
2 sprigs fresh parsley
juice of 1 lemon
1 red chilli pepper, chopped very small
1 tablespoon tahina
1 dessertspoon olive oil
1 dessertspoon water

Method

- In a wooden or earthenware mortar, mash the garlic clove, salt and fresh parsley. Add the lemon juice, chilli, tahina and water. Mix and stir in all these ingredients with a spoon to obtain a sauce of uniform consistency.
- Prepare the lumpy mdammas or the mdammas purée. The only difference between the two is that with the lumpy mixture, you don't mash all the cooked beans in the mortar. For the smooth purée, use a beater.
- If the beans are canned or preserved, heat them in a pan for five minutes, drain them and put them in a beater with half the sauce. Beat the mixture until it turns into a creamy, consistent purée. Turn the

purée out into a deep dish and cover it with the other half of the sauce. Sprinkle it with olive oil and accompany it with a raw, sliced onion. Mdammas *is eaten, as is* hommos, *with* eish *and directly from the dish. With the texture of Arab bread as mouldable as it is, people often substitute this for a fork or spoon to scoop food directly from the dish.*

بابا غنوج او متبل بيتنجان

MUTTABAL BETINJAN or BABA GANUJ
Aubergine purée

Perverter of women

This dish is one of a group of purées that differs from those already described, in that it is thought of strictly as a *meeza*, that is, an appetiser or starter. So it is served as often at lunch as at dinner, and almost never at breakfast time. It is very widespread in the Arab world, and of late, as with *falafel* and *hommos*, has been breaking frontiers the world over. This purée is known worldwide by the name of *muttabal betinjan*. However, in Syria and Palestine people know it by the aptly appropriate popular name of *baba ganuj* (Wanton coquette), doubtless because of its texture, which is as light as a ballerina, and for the insatiability it causes among those eating it.

In Syria and Palestine particularly, many mothers believe that this dish possesses the power to spread sweetness. They often give it to their daughters, believing they will acquire the same characteristics as the *baba ganuj*, that is, they will become provocative and wanton, two 'virtues' by which the Arab housewife is judged and which arouse fervour in the Arab male.

Within my own family, there exists a curious tale about this, which is at least as good as one you might find in any novel that goes under the name of magic realism. My aunt, the wife of my paternal uncle, a very credulous and at the

32

same time ingenuous woman, passed on her learning and her unshakable religious faith to her only daughter. For example, she forbade her, among other things, to eat this purée, in the hope that she would grow up serene, balanced and not remotely provocative. In fact, when the girl was fifteen, she looked thirty; she was as serene as she was shy, she never opened her mouth and rejected any boy intent on approaching her with sweet talk. My aunt died and my uncle remarried – this time a woman who originally came from Syria. She had only light religious convictions and was a great enthusiast of popular superstitions, believing blindly in the mysterious and marriageable properties of *baba ganuj*. And so she had no qualms about feeding her six daughters with this purée. It was soon apparent that the girls were growing up to possess an obvious and exaggerated coquetry, that awakened lust in any male. All of them were married before they reached the age of fifteen. Their mother's happiness was short lived. At the beginning of the 1980s, in the Muslim-Arab world, there was a strong surge of re-Islamisation, which left behind these six coquettish and irredentist women; 'naturally', they were divorced one after the other. And what was certain too was that their step-sister never married either, not even during this period, which undoubtedly offered the best opportunities for conservative women. Probably she had passed marriageable age. It was from this presumably that the comment originated among the womenfolk in our large family circle: 'When it comes to *baba ganuj*, you shouldn't have too little or too much.'

BABA GANUJ or MUTTABAL BETINJAN
Wanton coquette or Aubergine purée

Serves 4

Ingredients

2 large aubergines
1 teaspoon salt
5-6 dessertspoons tahina
2-3 cloves garlic
4-5 sprigs fresh parsley
juice of 1 medium lemon

Method

- *Prick the aubergines with a fork (3-4 pricks on each side of the aubergine).*
- *Roast the aubergines with their skins on, either under the grill or in the oven. Take them out when the skin is scorched. Leave them to cook, then peel them.*
- *While the aubergines are roasting, mash the peeled garlic, salt and parsley in a large mortar and mix in the lemon juice.*
- *Place the aubergines and the* tahina *in the mortar and gently mash the mixture over again to obtain a purée with a satisfactorily soft consistency.*
- *Serve in a deep dish, sprinkled with splashes of olive oil.*

VARIATIONS

The most interesting variation is the one the Lebanese call the *raheb* (the ascetic hermit). In this you omit the *tahina*, so the result is more modest and ascetic, as would befit a *raheb*.

Occasionally the dish is garnished with small pieces of tomato, onion, gherkins etc. Such a garnish cannot truly be described as a variation, but rather good taste or a personal choice.

MAGHREBI AUBERGINE PUREE

This is a very popular dish in North Africa. Except for the *tahina*, the rest of the ingredients are the same as in the recipe given above.

Peel a large aubergine, slice and season. Cook the slices for 30 minutes in a steamer, or a metal sieve placed in a saucepan of boiling water will do. Afterwards, heat the oil in a pan, using ½ cup of olive oil, and fry the slices of aubergine, together with the mashed garlic, a pinch of black pepper and also of paprika. Fry on a gentle flame, stirring and mashing all the ingredients until the whole is quite soft.

KIBBEH
Stuffed wheat croquettes

A wife's success or downfall

When my Syrian aunt (my father's brother's wife) was in the kitchen, I always watched her. She would be doing twenty things at once and yet manage to do them all and finish them: wash clothes, gossip with the neighbour through the window, tend to her daughters and so on. Perversely, she didn't give the slightest attention to the meal she was preparing that morning. It was a Friday and we usually ate *kibbeh*, a miserable dish for my mother to prepare, since she could never make it so well as the *bint el haram* (the daughter of sin), as she angrily called my aunt and, by extension, all Syrian and Lebanese women who were past masters in the art of making these croquettes.

Under my mother's instructions, I took notes, step by step, on how my aunt prepared the *kibbeh*, from the very first moment to the last, and not missing the smallest detail. My mother followed my notes to the letter, and proceeded to make some croquettes that were so disappointing that she never ever made them again.

Six years ago I was at my brother's home in Canada. I followed my Lebanese sister-in-law, step by step, as she made the *kibbeh*. Hers turned out to be perfect, and mine not. Why? Experts say that the vital secret lies in the hands and fingers of most of the women from these two nations. I have examined my Syrian cousins' fingers carefully, and those of my sister-in-law, her mother and various other women, and I've found nothing in the hands of those women that distinguishes them in any way from any other woman's. So you need a lot of imagination to swallow this theory ... though sometimes not too much, especially when you examine the difference between the croquettes some women make and the ones made by others. And of course, no Syrian or Lebanese has the slightest doubt of its veracity.

One of the most sought-after and flaunted virtues in the eyes of the family of a girl of marriageable age is her dexterity in preparing *kibbeh.* You frequently hear women discussing a new wife: '*Ma sha'a Allah* [Praise be to Allah], for from the fingers of this creation of His will come the best *kibbeh*s, and her husband will be powerless to reject her.'

When Rita Hayworth was married to the Ali Khan, Prince of the Ismaelites, she was harshly criticised by Lebanese women on account of her fingers. These, the women declared, were useless for making *kibbeh*, and furthermore augured a sad end to their marriage for both of them. Some might find parallels of this amusing anecdote in Don Quixote, who roundly praised certain women's hands for the way they could cure ham.

I confess that for some years now I've felt no urge to make these croquettes. It's thoroughly frustrating to hear some Lebanese or Syrian with minimal expertise in cooking first politely congratulate the cook for his *kibbeh*s and almost always – with reason – go on to list his flaws.

The following recipe is the most classic and the one most followed by Arab women, except the Syrians and Lebanese, who don't need any recipe to prepare their national dish *par excellence*. I wish you luck!

KIBBEH
Stuffed wheat croquettes

Makes 20

Ingredients

Outer layer

1 kg (2¼ lb) lamb, with no fat and minced very finely
1 kg (2¼ lb) burghul (cracked wheat)
2 tablespoons salt
1 tablespoon fulful bhar *(see p.206)*
1 tablespoon finely chopped onion
1 cup water

Stuffing

6 medium onions chopped very small (but not so finely as the onion for the outer coating)
500 grams (1 lb 2 oz) minced meat
1 cup samneh *or oil, for frying the meat (I prefer a mixture of both in equal parts)*
1 dessertspoon fulful bhar
1 dessertspoon salt
1 pinch of nutmeg
1 dessertspoon summak
150 grams (5 oz) of pine kernels (you can also add ground nuts)

3-5 cups of oil for frying the croquettes

Method

- To prepare the outer layer, mix all the ingredients to obtain a slightly flexible mixture. I advise you to put it through a mincer to obtain a fine, homogenous consistency. Set aside.
- To prepare the stuffing, heat the samneh and oil in a pan over a moderate flame and fry the pine kernels. Remove them from the pan and set aside.
- In the same oil, fry the onion and then mix in the meat and toss the mixture in the oil for 10 minutes, turning it continually. Season with all the spices and add the pine kernels. Remove from the pan.
- Divide the mixture for the outer covering into portions equal in size and shape to an egg. Place one portion in the palm of your hand and with your index finger or whatever of the other hand, indent it in the centre, at the same time turning the croquette so that you are enlarging the indentation, and leave it thus. Now here is where the skill of the cook is appreciated, for you must make all the croquettes uniformly of the same size and thickness, which should not be more than 40mm (1½ inches) across.
- Add some filling into the cavity and close it again, thus forming a croquette the size of a somewhat elongated egg.
- Repeat the same process with the rest of the mixture until you have finished it all.
- Heat 3-4 cups of oil in a relatively deep frying-pan and fry the croquettes until they are golden brown.
- Serve the croquettes hot, with yogurt, or on their own.

VARIATIONS

SENEYET KIBBEH

This is the *kibbeh* that is made in layers rather than as croquettes.

Grease an oven tray with *samneh* and place the outer layer mixture of the *kibbeh* in layers 75 mm (about 2½ inches) deep with a little of the stuffing between each layer. Bake.

This version of the original is very popular. And naturally enough it is made with unequal degrees of dexterity in all the countries of the fruitful moon.

KIBBEH JNOBIEH or KIBBEH SHIIEH
Southern kibbeh or Shiite kibbeh

This is the *kibbeh* that is made in the south of Lebanon. It is a very aromatic version, because included in the mixture for the outer layer and for the filling are varying quantities of very finely chopped dried leaves of two herbs, *marda kush* (sweet marjoram) and *ar-raihan* (myrtle) which both have powerful scents. These herbs, along with jasmine, cover a great part of the wooded countryside of Asia Minor, saturating it with their special fragrance.

KIBBEH NIYAH
Raw kibbeh

This is made all over the Middle East with the same ingredients and eaten raw.

KIBBEH IRAKIEH
Iraqi kibbeh

In this version the outer layer of the *kibbeh* is made with boiled potatoes instead of burghul and is stuffed with ingredients similar to those mentioned before, although in Iraq an infinite number of ingredients are used for the filling.

DIPS AND SALADS

In the Arab world there's so such thing as a sauce or a dressing as we understand them in the West. But the few 'sauces' and 'dressings' that one comes across in Arab gastronomy are included in this chapter on *salattet* (salads). They are more akin to dips and are considered as proper individual dishes that are complete in themselves. They are presented as accompaniments to other main dishes, or served on their own, with their own identity. You will frequently see an Arab fellow-diner asking for a dish of these 'dips' on their own and eating it with Arab bread which is used as a scoop. These dishes can be eaten at breakfast, lunch, dinner or at any time of day.

I am including in this chapter only the two best known 'dips', not only in Arab countries but in many others too.

LABAN MAA IJIAR
Cucumber with yogurt

All the countries in the eastern Mediterranean and Mesopotamia consider themselves copyright holders for the invention of this dip. I shall not enter into this unending dispute, but as long as the opposite remains unproved, I shall say that the Bedouin of Arabia were the first to prepare this food (so it appears from what is currently known), using fermented curdled milk as a base.

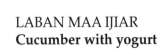

LABAN MAA IJIAR
Cucumber with yogurt

Serves 2

Ingredients

1 natural and 1 creamy yogurt (mixing the two will give the approximate flavour and consistency of the classic Arab yogurt).
1 medium cucumber or 2 small ones, peeled or half peeled and chopped very small. If the cucumber is large, you must put the slices in some butter muslin or a colander to get rid of the juice, squeezing them with your hands.
1 clove of garlic
1 teaspoon salt
2 fresh mint leaves
1 dessertspoon of dry, powdered mint
olive oil

Method

- *Crush the garlic, salt and fresh mint in a mortar.*
- *Mix them with the yogurt and cucumber in a deep bowl and add the dried mint. Mix again and sprinkle with little pools of olive oil.*

VARIATIONS

Many different versions of this 'dip' exist. The Egyptians add small slices of tomato and red chilli pepper. The Saudis add slices of various vegetables to the original mixture. The Palestinians, in addition to this original sauce, also make one with the same formula but omitting the cucumber. This is called *labinieh*.

BAADUNSEIH
Parsley with cream of sesame

Of this sauce we can say much the same as for the previous one. Nonetheless, in Arab gastronomy, two dishes exist that are always served with this particular sauce. They are *falafel* and *sayadeieh* (Boiled fish with rice).

BAADUNSEIH
Parsley with cream of sesame

Serves 2

Ingredients

1 teaspoon salt
1 clove garlic
½ cup of tahina
½ cup of water
½ cup of lemon juice
1 cup of very finely chopped fresh parsley

Method

- Put the salt and garlic in a mortar and crush them together. Add the tahina, *water and lemon juice. Mix well to obtain a kind of sauce with a texture similar to cream. Add the parsley and mix all the ingredients together again.*
- *Serve in a bowl or deep plate.*

VARIATIONS

Sometimes the parsley is omitted to make a version called *taratur* (Near East), which is used to accompany *falafel* or *kafta* (minced meat roasted on a tray in the oven).

There is another, highly regarded version in the Arabian Gulf countries, called *salata bi tahina* (salad with *tahina*), in which small quantities of the tiniest pieces of tomato, gherkins and chillis are added to the original sauce. This is eaten a lot as an accompaniment to grilled or fried fish.

TABBOULEH
Special burghul salad

Erotic undertones

Tabbouleh is thought of as a starter or, more accurately, an appetiser. In contrast to the starters or hors d'oeuvre served at a Western meal, which are served first and then withdrawn, *tabbouleh* remains permanently on the table, so that the diner can from time to time go on picking at it, for the saying goes that it possesses a kind of magical power to stimulate the appetite for the other main dishes.

The Arabs attribute a great deal of importance to the appetisers in their meals, especially when there are guests. The Arab host can relax when he sees his guests tucking into the dishes he's served them. Eating a great deal in the Arab world is indicative of generosity on the part of the person doing it. When a guest shows a large appetite and gratification for the meal, this is seen as a visible sign of his 'willing' obligation to do his utmost to return that feeling of gratification to his host, when it becomes the host's turn to be the guest.

If the opposite of this happens and the guest shows little enthusiasm for the food being served, then he will be criticised for being stingy and miserable, for eating only a small amount implies to the host that, when their roles are reversed and he in turn is invited to his guest's house, he too should eat only a little.

If you, as a guest from a foreign country, are invited to a banquet or dinner at an Arab's house, then it is definitely not a waste of time to give serious consideration to the following advice. Go to the feast ravenously hungry, chew slowly, serve yourself small portions (for the host will continuously bombard you with food without asking). Try out each dish and get the measure of it: this way you will be able to go on taking more helpings of the ones you like, until you can't eat a thing more. Also you have to try to be one of the last to finish the meal. *Tabbouleh* is a great help to the guest in achieving this objective.

Tabbouleh has very ancient origins. It is known that it was made before the time of the Umayyads and was known in Al-Andalus and in various regions of the Mediterranean. (The Umayyads were an Arabic dynasty who ruled from Damascus in the seventh and eighth centuries. They were deposed by the Abbassides and moved to Cordoba in Spain, where they founded a second dynasty which lasted until the eleventh century. Al-Andalus was the name given to Moorish Spain.) *Tabbouleh* was made at that time with the same ingredients that are used today. We know that it is a dish that originated in Syria, and the exact location was around Aleppo and Damascus, although it has to be said that the Lebanese are the true masters in its preparation. When made correctly, it should not be like a sort of mixed salad with a bit of burghul. It was some Syrians who hit on the idea to *en tabal* (season or adorn) the whole with spices and lemon, and since this mixture is served on individual little plates, it's called by this diminutive, festive and witty name.

In the Arab world, the verb *tabal* and the noun *tabbouleh* can have various meanings and, for example, lend themselves to much erotic word play. This was made popular in a series of playful, frivolous and well known songs, which praise and suggest the sensation of pleasure which eating *tabbouleh* induces. And there was a very famous Lebanese singer called N. Salam, who sang provocatively to her lover:

> *Here, let yourself go*
> *I'm making you* tabbouleh
> *And a cup of coffee*
> *And we shall be in heaven.*

As is well known Arab coffee is infused with cardamom, a potent aphrodisiac. It seems that among the Lebanese there exists a tacit agreement that people who neither make nor eat *tabbouleh* are irredeemably dull.

TABBOULEH
Special burghul salad

Serves 4

Ingredients

1 full cup of semolina or burghul
1 handful (200 grams [7 oz]) parsley
500 grams (just over 1 lb) raw tomato
1 handful (100 grams [4 oz]) fresh mint
2 large onions
1 cup of virgin olive oil
juice of 2 medium lemons
1 dessertspoon salt
1 teaspoon of a mixture in equal parts of cumin, black pepper and cinnamon

Method

- *Wash and strain the burghul. Add the lemon juice and set aside.*
- *Wash and drain the parsley and mint, and chop them very, very finely*
- *Cut up the tomatoes and the onions into very tiny slivers (almost mashed). Mix them with the salt, pepper, cumin and cinnamon.*
- *Mix together all the above ingredients and add the oil.*
- *Serve the* tabbouleh *on small individual plates, or pile it on large, individual lettuce leaves.*

الفتوش

FATTUSH
Salad with croutons

This is a delicious salad, which is easy to prepare and is considered a rival to *tabbouleh*.

FATTUSH
Salad with croutons

Serves 2

Ingredients

1 tomato
1 cucumber
1 green pepper
gherkins
lettuce
a few olives
onion
2 tablespoons oil
1 tablespoon lemon juice

1 tablespoon vinegar
1 tablespoon finely chopped fresh parsley
1 teaspoon salt
1 teaspoon dried mint
small pieces of bread
samneh *(see glossary)*

Method

- *Prepare a normal salad with tomato, cucumber, green pepper, gherkins, lettuce, some olives and onion. Season with oil, lemon juice, vinegar and parsley. Add salt and sprinkle with dried mint.*
- *In the Arab world no food is ever wasted, and everything is put to good use, in this case,* fatte *– hard crusts and pieces of dry Arab bread. Fry the* fatte *in a pan with a bit of* samneh *(never oil) and a pinch of salt. When they are golden brown, take them out of the pan and add them to the salad.*
- *Mix all the ingredients and serve at once; in this way, the bits of bread will be crunchy and won't go soggy or lose their original flavour.*

SUGGESTION

As you savour these dishes, envelop yourself in the velvety voice of the Lebanese singer Fayruz; their flavour will truly acquire another dimension.

MAIN COURSES

These are the so-called basic dishes in the Arab world. In the West and in other cultures it's customary to present a mild dish as a starter, a second more substantial dish and finally a third rich main course. Then, the guests comment on the different dishes they have consumed. In contrast, in the Arab world, only the main dish is ever referred to, although numerous other dishes may have accompanied it. So, when faced with the classic question that Arabs ask: 'What did you have to eat at So-and-so's?', the reply always only ever mentions the main course and totally ignores the rest.

The main dishes contain details of unequivocal significance that betray the status of the guest as much as of the host. Traditionally, an Arab always automatically offers the best dishes to a stranger, and the non-fulfilment of this duty is unforgivable. On the other hand, he does not harbour the same feelings for and with his own family and friends.

It is not looked upon kindly if a host of limited means offers an extraordinary, special dish to a rich acquaintance of his, but, on the other hand, it would be considered a noble gesture of outstanding generosity if he did so to a poor man or to a friend of equal social standing. With the rich the opposite is true: it is not looked upon kindly if a rich man offers a great feast to his friends, acquaintances or family whose socio-economic status happens to be inferior, because such a gesture could easily be interpreted as insulting exhibitionism and ostentation.

MJADARAH
Rice with lentils

A dish with many meanings

Mjadarah is actually a dish of Persian origin that was well known in medieval times under other names. Nowadays, it is also known by different names depending on which region or country you are in; for example, in Egypt it's called *kushary*, and in Syria, *mudardara*...This dish is also made with slight variations in non-Arab countries of the Mediterranean.

Mjadarah is, *par excellence,* the poor man's dish. It became popular in the Arab world in the 1940s and 1950s as a consequence of continuous wars and emigration. The fact that the raw materials for it are easy to keep and transport helped spread it, especially in times of social conflict and war. The Palestinians, because of their status as refugees and the fact that they are permanently on the move, were the ones truly responsible for making and spreading this dish in the Arab world. The United Nations consolidated this move through its aid to Palestinian refugees of non-perishable food, which consisted of the main ingredients for *mjadarah*: rice and lentils.

A guest at an Arab meal would never be guest of honour with a plate of *mjadarah*: such an offering would be seen as an insult. However, if the guest asked his host, quite specifically and ahead of time, if he could have a plate of *mjadarah*, it would signify mutual confidence, a plea for austerity and a tacit confession of humility on the part of the guest. I recall from my travels in the Near East the perplexity etched in the faces of my hosts when I asked for this dish in advance. As we all know, people who return to their country of origin after a long absence always feast themselves on nostalgic food for which they have a sudden urge, usually traditional dishes.

The Arab host, in this case a conscientious one, is conscious of his guest's longing and sense of loss and for his sake accedes to his whim, but in no case is the Arab proverb forgotten which says: ' The Arab's nobility can be detected in the meal he offers his guest.' So, if by any chance, he were to serve *mjadarah*, it would be seen as a marginal dish or an eccentric one among a plethora of other varied dishes.

In all sincerity, behind closed doors, *mjadarah* is not a secondary dish, but the main course and normal food for an immense majority of the Arab population.

This dish has frequently been used for political ends by some petty Arab leader who wants to gain favour with the masses. So you can often see Arab leaders publicly airing their 'humility' by eating a plate of *mjadarah*.

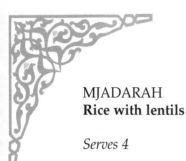

MJADARAH
Rice with lentils

Serves 4

Ingredients

200 grams (7 oz) dried lentils
100 grams (4 oz) rice, preferably long grain
2 tablespoons samneh *(see glossary)*
1 dessertspoon salt
1 pinch of cumin
3 medium onions, chopped very small
3 cups water

Method

- *Pour the water into a medium-sized saucepan over a high flame and add the lentils that have previously been washed. When the water begins to boil, reduce the heat to minimum and leave to cook for 30 minutes.*
- *Immediately add the salt, cumin and rice (this should have been thoroughly rinsed in water two or three times). Mix well and cook over the same heat as before for a further 20 minutes.*
- *Meanwhile, lightly fry the onion with the* samneh *in a pan until it is golden brown.*
- *Add the onion to the saucepan and mix all the contents together again. Cook over a low heat for a further 5 minutes. Withdraw it from the fire and leave it to rest.*

SUGGESTIONS

Mjadarah is eaten on its own, with natural yogurt, or Arab-style salad. Basically they are the same prime ingredients, but chopped very finely. Add lemon juice, salt, vinegar, virgin olive oil, some wisps of dried mint and mix all together well.

I recommend stirring the dried lentils in water with a spoonful of baking powder for 1 hour before you cook them.

VARIATIONS

SALATET RUZZ WA ADAS
Rice with hot lentils

This variation is very well known in the Maghreb region. The Maghrebs cook the lentils and rice in separate saucepans in boiling water, drain them, then mix them together in a large bowl. Then they incorporate the onions seasoned with the spices and previously tossed in butter over a low heat to soften them. Finally, they garnish it with small chunks of raw onion on top.

AR-RUZZ
Rice

The feast of San Juan and the Emir

The great Confucius once said that 'A feast without rice would be like a splendid woman with one eye missing'. Arabs and followers of Confucius share similar beliefs on many issues, but on this one about rice they are in complete and utter agreement. The visitor who travels the Arab world from east to west and from north to south will come to understand that not even a half-decent feast can take place without rice.

'Eat up that rice,' our elders would urge us. 'That way you'll grow up strong and have lots of children,' my grandmother used to insist. Bearing in mind that the old woman had never been outside Palestine, not even outside her village, and that in the whole of her long life she had read no book other than the Koran, I have often wondered where she got this idea from. She would have known absolutely nothing about the ancient religious Hindu practice of showering newly weds with rice as a symbol to insure fertility. I really don't know if it is down to the rice or not, but one thing is certain: that Arabs and Indians occupy first place among the nations of the world as far as fertility goes, and will continue to do so until the advent of McDonald's.

In fact, as a way to overcome our overwhelming money problems, our mothers found in rice a complete diet that was simultaneously filling and very cheap. Time and time again they would say: 'You must eat rice every day, because it contains *fusfor* (phosphorus) which gives you intelligence, and *potas* (potassium), which is very relaxing.' Curiously, as a result of eating so much rice, it was the potassium that affected us much more than the phosphorus, for we were always napping.

I remember an episode involving my professor of medicine. He was as stubborn and as obstinate as a mule when it came to academic work. My fellow students begged him to postpone the day scheduled for a practical exam. We were overwhelmed with so many exams and other assignments all taking place in a very short space of time. This professor had – and still has – a very great weakness for Eastern cooking. My friends suggested to me that he be invited to a copious and 'relaxing' Arab spread, on the same day and just a few hours before the exam. And so the professor, enchanted by the invitation, came to my lodgings at the pre-arranged time, at two in the afternoon, three hours before the exam. I remember that I prepared a great pot of *maqlouba* (see page 73). The professor had helping after helping of this savoury rice to the point where he could not get up from the floor where we were sitting, Arab fashion, to eat. And there, on that very spot, he fell asleep. The following day our illustrious guest, who was truly as cunning as the devil himself, and who had, undaunted, put up with our prank, fixed a new date for the exam – the 24 June – the feast day of San Juan and of Catalonia, and the day following the open air celebrations, during which rivers of sparkling Cava are drunk and tons of free food eaten, thousands of fireworks released and hundreds of street bonfires set alight. In a nutshell, with so much merriment that night, no one could reconcile himself to sleep. And this is exactly what happened to us that night.

Naturally, the following day, none of us turned up for the exam, and, naturally, the professor suspended the lot of us.

Centuries ago, the Arabs grew crops of rice and spread its use in all parts of the world, but in spite of this, all the Arab countries, except Egypt, imported it, and always have done, from outside. In fact there were periods in which not even Egypt enjoyed better luck than her Arab brothers, for a great part of her rice was taken from her by the big colonialist countries.

At the beginning of the twentieth century, the serving of rice on its own was a luxury and a symbol of the status or generosity of the host. Several decades later, rice's status underwent a decline, due to important socio-economic factors. On the one hand, there were various wars in the region which had dire consequences; one of the gravest of these was the appearance of waves of refugees who were suffering from starvation. The most practical way to help them was to send produce, such as rice, which was non-perishable and resistant to the inclemencies of climate and transport. Along with lentils this became the main food for refugees. Also during that same period (1950-60), Egypt was obtaining her independence and immediately made use of the produce from her huge rice fields. Anglo-French colonialism did not take kindly to the loss of its dominion over the country of the Nile, and the Western world blocked Egypt's main exports, especially rice and cotton. As a consequence, Egypt sought an outlet for her produce but was only able to do business with Arab merchants, who were then inundated with Egyptian rice, albeit of great quality and very cheap. The abundance and the low price of the rice caused a lowering of its prestige among the general public.

My mother's recriminations against my sisters were frequent as they rejected their daily intake of rice for fear of getting fat. Totally unaware of the fashions, my mother would say to them sarcastically: 'You can turn your nose up at this saying, but if only you knew. There were times when the Sultan of Istanbul, his very self, yearned even for a teaspoonful of rice.' In fact, during the First World War, almost all the Near East was under Ottoman (Turkish) domination. Using general mobilisation as an excuse, they plundered the *wilayat* (provinces) of their resources as much for food as for people (men between the ages of 14 and 60 were forced to enlist in the Ottoman army). And as if that were not enough, there were also at that time some terrible plagues of locusts which razed everything – tender or tough – from the fields. My grandmother, in her primitive language, used to tell me about how it was then. 'Day after day, we were in a permanent solar eclipse – and in full summer,' was how she described the sky darkened with clouds of locusts. At the same time, everything was in short supply. People were eating grass, dates…they became very inventive at preparing stews made basically from grass and water, and on rare occasions with a bit of salt and onion. So, then, having a bit of rice or wheat to hand was synonymous with great luxury, and from that stemmed my mother's – possibly exaggerated – annoyance.

Rice can be prepared in a thousand ways. There are various types of rice: long grain, round, short, rice that has been sprayed, rice with added vitamins etc. Each type will behave differently during the cooking procedure. Throughout this modest book, I have tried to simplify to the maximum methods of preparing various recipes. Here too I'm following the same line and will leave to others better informed than myself to explain the thousand and one features of rice.

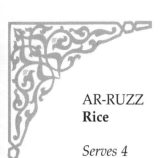

AR-RUZZ
Rice

Serves 4

Ingredients

500 grams (just over 1 lb) white, long-grain rice (approximately 2 large cups of rice)
2 cups of sieved chicken or meat stock (the quantity should be the same as the rice)

Method

- *Authentic Arab rice is prepared using just these two ingredients. Put the stock in a saucepan of medium depth and turn the heat up high.*
- *Meanwhile, wash the rice 3-4 times in water and drain.*
- *Throw the rice into the stock, making sure that it is evenly spread. At the end of 5 minutes, turn the heat down to minimum and continue cooking for 10-12 minutes or until all the liquid has been totally absorbed by the rice.*
- *Withdraw it from the heat and leave it to rest for 3-5 minutes. Serve immediately, hot.*

SUGGESTIONS

Real stock is not always available, in which case substitute water. Put the water over a fierce heat and add a table-spoonful of *samneh,* a dessertspoonful of salt, and a pinch of powdered saffron or turmeric. Once these have dis-solved in the water, which will take on a light yellow colour, follow the remaining steps of the recipe above. In fact, this is the rice people eat every day and is made at home throughout the Arab world. Now, at banquets, events or simply at an infrequent party among friends, this classic rice, which is made as often with stock as it is with water, will, when it is served, be garnished with a topping of almonds and pine kernels (a Jordanian and Palestinian speciality), or raisins (Iraqi), or pistachios (Syrian), or minced meat (Egyptian and Sudanese), or raisins and plums (Tunisian, Moroccan and Algerian), or with lightly fried minced meat and roasted or crushed cardamom (Yemeni).

There was a time when it was rumoured that some prince of one of the rich Gulf States used to sprinkle his rice with gold dust. I have not seen this for myself. But knowing how eccentric the emirs can be, it would not surprise me. I know one of the thousands of Arab emirs who swarm all over the globe (I would like to say that it's no great achievement meeting one) who was admitted to the hospital where I was working. He was a great drinker and, as you know, patients admitted to hospital cannot drink a drop of alcohol, nor can doctors allow them to. The emir sent his private nurse to buy him various bottles of the best perfumes that there were on the market, which, so it was said, were presents for the nurses in the hospital. But, come the end of a week, by which time the private nurse had bought dozens of flasks of perfume, not a single nurse in the hospital had received one. It was precisely this last detail which brought out into the open the emir's alcoholic eccentricity. You can imagine what our prince had done with all those bottles of perfume! Every day he had drunk the contents of a good few along with some ice cubes. In the hospital the doctors drew his attention, in friendly fashion, to the dangers of the ingredients. He grunted and assured us that there was nothing special to worry about because 'My countrymen and I acquired this habit every time the government acted tough and increased their vigilance on alcohol, but fortunately the excessive zeal of our wise and most merciful government never used to last very long.'

To end, it's certainly a well known fact that all those 'champions of Islam', the countries of the Arabian Gulf, are the greatest importers of perfume in the world.

الشاكرية

SHAKRIEH
Thanksgiving

A children's favourite

Shakrieh is the name by which this dish is known in most Arab countries. In olden times, depending on which region you belonged to, you would hear different variations in the stories about it, but they were all in agreement as to how it was so named. It comes from this dish's thanksgiving for the relative abundance of its main ingredient of yogurt, made from fresh goat or camel milk.

For centuries past and right up to the present day, the Arab world has suffered continually from violent changes, due to both political and natural causes, of which the irremediable consequences are misery and food shortages. Almost always up until the mid twentieth century, there was some milk-producing animal in the vast majority of homes and, since then, in situations of poverty, they have had recourse to them. An infinite number of products have been made from animals' milk, and one of them is yogurt. People add to the yogurt, salt, water and a small amount of onion, heat it up a little and it's ready to eat. At the end of the meal they say, *'Shukran li Allah'* (Thanks be to Allah) for the existence of this ingredient. In other words, *Shakrieh* comes from *shukura* (thanks). This is the most common explanation of the origin of the dish's name. The Druses and some Lebanese Christians don't emphatically deny this version of the origin of this dish, but they give it the name of *laban immuh* (mother's milk). On numerous occasions, I've heard mothers recommending this or that person to make use of this infallible alternative of *shakrieh* for apathetic or stubborn children who habitually have eating problems. Certainly in Europe, I follow this same theory and offer this dish to my guests' children who have never refused to eat it. In the same way, a Bedouin from Saudi Arabia insists that it is called *shakrieh,* because *'Nashkur* (we give thanks) to Allah and the dish which is, when all is said and done, a "happy event" from God Almighty, in that it has saved our children from not eating properly'.

Because of improvements in the economic situation of the Arab world, the original recipe has undergone a number of modifications. Today people can add meat and spices to the *shakrieh.*

SHAKRIEH
Thanksgiving

Serves 4

Ingredients

5 natural yogurt, or approximately ¾ litre or 1⅓ pints of yogurt
1 cup of water
1 medium onion chopped small
1 egg
300 grams (10 oz) minced meat (coarsely minced)
2-3 tablespoons olive oil
½ level teaspoon fulful bhar *(see p.260)*
½ teaspoon cinnamon
1 teaspoon salt
1 tablespoon lemon juice

Method

- *Put the oil in a pan over moderate heat. After a couple of minutes, add the onion. When it has become transparent, add the meat, salt and the* fulful bhar. *Stir continuously until it is cooked. Set aside.*
- *Tip the yogurt, water, lemon juice and raw egg (minus shell) into a saucepan of medium depth over gentle heat. Stir the contents with a wooden spoon continuously for 5 minutes. Add the lightly fried meat and continue stirring for 5 more minutes. Turn off the heat.*
- *Turn the contents of the saucepan into a crystal dish, preferably green or brown, and dust the whitish mixture with cinnamon. This way the dish takes on a more varied, sensuous colouring.*

SUGGESTIONS

Shakrieh is always served along with a plate of white rice and is eaten by mixing a spoonful of *shakrieh* with one of rice. This dish is a children's favourite, but it is not exclusively a children's dish, adults also very much enjoy it.

VARIATIONS

HALIB or LABAN IMMOH
Mother's milk

This Syrian-Lebanese version adds chunks of meat (as for a stew) rather than minced meat.

MANSAF

I would like to include here (and I hope no Jordanian will read this) the national Jordanian dish *par excellence*. This is *mansaf*. It is of Bedouin origin and is made basically from the same ingredients as *shakrieh*: lamb cut into pieces, rice and sour yogurt (*jmid*, yogurt balls). Using their hands, the Bedouin mould the yogurt (made from goat's milk) into balls which can be kept over a long period of months or even years. This recipe poses certain problems, as the dish has a very strong taste for the Western palate, and if I explain how it ought to be eaten, my feeling is that you will end up resisting any temptation to make it yourself. *Mansaf* is eaten with the hands directly from a large communal platter, in which the three basic ingredients are cooked and mixed. You get hold of a handful of cooked yogurt and rice and mould it in the palm of your hand, like pastry, into a soft ball...then you pop it into your mouth. And you continue with this procedure until you can't eat any more. It has a flavour similar to *shakrieh* but much stronger. The Bedouin are traditionally very indulgent towards their foreign guests and always offer you a spoon. But it would be a grand gesture towards the Bedouin if you were to refuse the spoon and eat like the rest.

MAACARONA
Macaroni

...And the Libyan Revolution

We arrived in Libya one suffocating August afternoon. I had gone there with a group of fellow Arab students who were also studying in Europe, in the hope of meeting up with thousands more students from other parts of the world. The venues were conferences held in aid of Palestine, and convoked after Libya's recent, triumphant revolution.

Libya at that time lacked any distinctive stamp as it is a curious anomaly (being neither completely Maghrebi, nor Near Eastern, nor African). After the death of Nasser (the undisputed leader of what was then the Third World), Libya made an (unsuccessful) bid to lead the Third World and Arabs in general. The Libyans were endlessly organising conferences, meetings, summits, international congresses etc, all with the same anti-colonial, Pan-Arab, Third World stance.

During the course of the conferences, there were many discussions and debates. And, if our questions to the fathers of the revolution were impertinent (we were adolescent), their replies were most certainly loaded with surrealism. I remember one of the most entertaining. A very young Yemini reproached a revolutionary braggart who was tormenting us with a Pan-Arabist peroration, because he was encouraging the audience to rely on national produce, while, throughout his speech, he was chain-smoking tobacco produced by North American imperialists. This particular 'revolutionary', however, was completely unfazed by this taunt and quick off the mark. 'Watch me,' he told the unruly Yemeni as he lit yet another cigarette – 'I'm burning that imperialism to ashes.' There was sonorous applause.

'And why should you Libyans, so many years after gaining independence from Italian colonialism, still be using macaroni – when it's a genuinely Italian product – as the basis for your most popular dishes?' asked a Sudanese. 'Genuinely Italian?' the revolutionary questioned angrily. 'You're all so ignorant,' he went on. 'The whole world is ignorant. Macaroni never originated in Italy. It came from China, and we Arabs, our forebears, were the ones who brought pasta to Sicily and Naples. So we, the revolutionaries', he added very emphatically, 'we must eat more macaroni, so we can rightfully reclaim its Chinese and Arabic origins for ourselves.'

Except for the Chinese student delegates, who were totally disconcerted by this assertion, the rest of the gathering rose from their seats, applauding and wildly acclaiming Mao and Gadaffi who, according to those present, were the true saviours, for having recaptured macaroni from the dark dungeons of imperialism.

Despite his verbal diarrhoea and his diatribes, what the speaker had said about macaroni's origin made sense and was absolutely true.[2]

So, though these conferences, like many others which took place in Arab countries, were in principle dedicated to saving Palestine, the only thing that was finally saved for certain was macaroni.

Over the seven days in which the revolutionary conferences took place, the Libyans filled us to the gills with *chakchouka* (a kind of sainfoin with eggs), couscous, and numerous different versions of macaroni – of which the best known is *mbakbaka*.

MBAKBAKA
Macaroni

Serves 3-4

Ingredients

500 grams (1 lb 2oz) macaroni
750 grams (1½ lb lamb or veal), washed thoroughly and cut into bite sized pieces
3 large onions, chopped very finely or sliced
4-5 tablespoons olive oil
1 tablespoon salt
1 tablespoon fulful bhar *(see p.206)*
500 grams (just over 1 lb) ripe tomatoes, peeled and chopped fairly small
1 tablespoon shatta *or* harissa *(both are available in specialist shops, and* harissa *is now available in large supermarkets)*

Method

- *Cook the macaroni in a saucepan in boiling salted water.*
- *Meanwhile, in a frying pan lightly fry the onions in oil over a moderate heat.*
- *Once they are golden, add the meat, salt, and the* fulful bhar. *Continue cooking and when the meat is well cooked and tender, add the tomatoes and the peppery spice. Mix all the ingredients in the pan,*

and continue cooking for 5 more minutes.

- *Strain the macaroni and put it back in the saucepan.*
- *Put the saucepan over a gentle heat and incorporate the mixture from the pan. Stir and cook for a further 10 minutes, stirring every so often with a wooden spoon to avoid the macaroni sticking together.*
- *Withdraw from the heat and serve on a large deep plate.*

VARIATIONS

In the Arab world and in Libya especially there are a great many versions of macaroni dishes.

MBAKBAKA BI TOMEH
Macaroni with garlic (Libya)

This is the same recipe as the one given above, but substituting fresh garlic for the onions.

SENEYET MAACARONA
Macaroni baked in the oven (Near East)

In a saucepan of boiling water, semi-cook the macaroni and then transfer them to a baking dish. Add 250 grams (9 oz) of minced meat and onion (both lightly fried in a little oil, until half done), and a discreet quantity of *fulful bhar* (see p.206) and salt. Mix all these ingredients together well with a spoon and make them into a flat layer. Finally pour into the baking dish a sauce made up of 2½ cups of water and peeled and grated raw tomato, in equal portions. The sauce should cover the macaroni mixture entirely.

Put the baking dish in the oven at 180-200°C (350-400°F, gas 4-6), and remove it when the liquid has been totally absorbed by the macaroni, or when it is all cooked.

MAACARONE KAZZABEH
Mock macaroni

MAACARONE HAF
Dry macaroni

MAACARONE KAHLEH
Desert macaroni

All these are euphemisms that indicate, obviously, that the meat, the most valued ingredient in a dish, has been omitted. It is very difficult for an outsider ever to see this dish, because Arabs entertain their guests so well and would never serve them a main dish that did not contain meat.

But, be in no doubt, these dishes are made extensively throughout the Arab world and are frequently produced at home – behind closed doors – among the most underprivileged strata of society.

MAACARONA BI LABAN
Macaroni with yogurt

Serves 2

Ingredients

150 grams (5 oz) macaroni
1 peeled garlic
1 tablespoon salt
50 grams (2 oz) fresh parsley
1 sprig coriander
1 pinch fulful bhar (see p.206)
2 natural yogurt (1 creamy, 1 normal)

Method

- *Boil the macaroni in a saucepan with boiling water. Drain and reserve.*
- *In a bowl, pound together the garlic, salt, parsley, coriander and the fulful bhar. Add the yogurt and mix all the contents of the bowl together well until you obtain a creamy and homogenous sauce.*
- *Add this to the macaroni and mix again.*

SUGGESTIONS

We thoroughly recommend this dish, particularly in summer. Serve it cold and garnished with sprigs of fresh parsley. Occasionally, the dish is garnished with fried minced meat and pine kernels sautéed over a moderate heat with a pinch of salt and butter.

MAQLOUBA
Topsy-turvy

Accompanied by the diva, Um Kulthum

On numerous occasions when we've been eating this dish, my European friends have asked me what it's called. I've never heard a proper name for it in any European language. Often I get round it by saying it's called 'Arab paella'. And everyone accepts this approximation unquestioningly. In fact, I'm not too far off the mark. Paella – probably a noun of Arabic origin (*paqui, pailla*) – means 'remains'. What was left over (*paquia*) from the lavish tasty Arab dishes from the tables of Caliphs, Emirs or simply rich citizens was given to the servants and the poor. Muslims never waste or throw away any food, since it is a gift from Allah.

The history of *maqlouba* (Arab paella) is not much different from that of Valencian paella, except for its contents. Originally, according to what my maternal grandmother told me (she was born in 1870, and seemingly in a well-off family), on Fridays, a sacred feast day for Muslims, she used to cook something good. The leftovers of the meal were then put together in a cooking pot to await the arrival of the first poor people. She didn't let them have the cooking pot as it would have been very difficult for them to eat out of it directly, and instead chose to empty it out on to an enormous tray. She would lift up the cooking pot and to surprise and impress those needy people, she would let the contents slide out very slowly to form a compact mound. It was presumably from this tipping-up of the dish that its name, Topsy-turvy, or *maqlouba*, came.

My grandmother told me that she was following the same custom as her mother, and she, in turn, her antecedents etc. etc. going right back to the time of the Abbassides caliphs (who ruled from Baghdad from 750 to 1285).[3]

Nowadays *maqlouba* is not simply made up of leftovers, nor is it just for the poor. It is now a respectable and noted dish and one which is served on special, festive occasions.

MAQLOUBA
Topsy-turvy

Serves 4

Ingredients

500 grams (just over 1 lb) aubergine
500 grams (just over 1 lb) lamb or chicken (lamb is better), cut up as for a stew
8 cups water
1 tablespoon salt
50 grams (2 oz) pine kernels
50 grams (2 oz) raw almonds
300 grams (10 oz) rice (long grain is best)
100 grams (4 oz) butter (Arab butter is best – you can find it in Middle Eastern stores)
1 teaspoonful fulful bhar *(see p.206)*
½ level teaspoon saffron
2-3 cups oil for frying the aubergines

Method

- *Peel the aubergines. Cut them into long or round slices, no more than 1 cm (⅖ inch) thick and fry them over a moderate heat. Put them on a plate on a piece of kitchen towel to soak up any surplus oil.*
- *Wash the lamb or chicken thoroughly and boil it up in a cooking pot over a moderate heat. Remove any scum which it produces, add the spices and salt, and cover. Cook for 30 minutes and afterwards separate the meat from the broth.*
- *Wash the rice several times and drain.*
- *Grease another cooking pot, which is not so deep, with a little butter. In this pot, juxtapose the ingredients in layers. On the first and lowest put the meat you've already cooked, then the fried aubergines and finally, spread the rice over the top as the last layer.*
- *Finally, pour over a quantity of the broth from the hot meat gradually so as not to disturb the top layer, so that it covers the three layers by about 2 cm (⅖ inch).*
- *Cover and cook over a high heat for the first 5 minutes. Then, turn down the heat to minimum and cook for a further 25-30 minutes.*
- *Turn off the heat and wait for 2 minutes for the food to rest. Remove the lid from the pot and exchange it for a bigger, flat dish. Invert the pot on to the dish, as if it were a flan. Lift it slowly and the contents will appear in their traditional shape (like a flan).*
- *Sprinkle over some pine kernels and almonds which have been fried in butter until golden brown.*
- *Serve the* maqlouba *just as it is, with yogurt and Arab salad. It is usually eaten with a slightly creamy yogurt.*

A special recommendation from a Libyan cook:

While you're preparing this meal and eating it, immerse yourself pleasurably in the voice of Um Kulthum. The voice of this *set* (diva) singing in the Arab world, mingled with the aroma of the butter, spices and golden brown nuts will at once transport you to the banks of the Nile and the Jordan, to the little alleyways and arched passageways of

Jerusalem and Damascus. In other words, while you're in your kitchen, your mind will be riding on a camel across the bare dunes of the desert from a thousand and one Arabian nights. I confess that I've always followed this recommendation, and played the song called *Ghanni-li shwayye shwayye* (Pleasure me and sing to me), which goes

Sing to me slowly and in exchange	غنيلي شوية شوية
I offer you my eyes.	غنيلي وخذ عيني
Song is the soul's life-giving rain	المغنى حياة الروح
Curing the patient, healing the wound.	يسمعها العليل يشفيه

VARIATION

Maqlouba with cauliflower is a traditional country people's dish. Townspeople tend to be more select and prefer aubergines, because cauliflower gives off a smell that isn't all that pleasant.

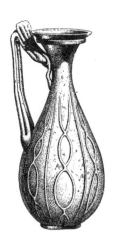

SAYADEIEH
Fish with rice

An antipathy for fish

Many Western historians will tell you that the Arabs were never great seafarers. I mentioned this piece of nonsense at a social gathering of some Iraqi friends and one of them commented: 'Oh, these *faranjas*.[4] Ask those know-alls where Sinbad the Sailor came from.'

Knowing whether or not they were great sailors is not really at issue, but what I was interested in finding out was why in Arab gastronomy, ever since ancient times, have there been so few recipes for fish? There are various reasons to explain this. For one, religious reasons, since 15 per cent of Muslims are of the Shi-ite faith that observes certain prohibitions and reservations with regard to many species of marine fauna. For example, they don't eat prawns, their argument being that prawns and various other sea creatures feed on the waste of others; or put in a nutshell, there's little difference between them and pigs. This prohibition causes some confusion among Suni (Orthodox) Muslims, so that many of them tend to choose the easiest option and not eat fish at all, even though it is not prohibited. The *hdedu*, who live in the Atlas Mountains, do not accept fish, and will not even so much as taste any in general.

Other reasons are technological, for owing to the hot

weather in this region, the transport of fish and keeping it afterwards is complicated.

Finally, another reason rests in the idiosyncrasy of the Arab who, since olden times, is as a general rule, not enthusiastic about foraging for his family blindly and at random. It is much more secure to have a flock of animals on *terra firma* and not on (or under) a shifting surface (Arabs are afraid of the sea). The first option allows for the head of a household to be near his own children; the second does not. The Arab will always have a preference for the former.

For all these reasons, consumption of most of the fish (which nonetheless amounts to a great deal) in Arab countries is concentrated in their coastal regions. On the coast it is customary to eat fried or grilled fish, and on rare occasions, boiled or baked. Of the stewed dishes, we highlight one here which is very famous on almost all the coasts of the Arab world and that is *sayadeieh* (Fisherwoman).

SAYADEIEH
Fish with rice

Serves 4

Ingredients

2 cups of rice
1 kg (2¼ lb) of fish (of good quality)
½ dessertspoon fulful bhar *(see p.206)*
1 dessertspoon salt

Method

- *Put the rice in soak for 30 minutes.*
- *Place the fish in a large saucepan with sufficient water to cover it, and bring it to the boil. Add the spices and salt. When the fish is half cooked, remove it from the saucepan (reserving the stock). Remove the bones and cut it up into pieces.*
- *Wash the rice three or four times.*
- *Place half the fish in a flat-bottomed pan to form the first layer. Then spread half the rice on top, then add the other half of the fish, and finally the rest of the rice. So you will have four layers in the pan, one on top of the other.*
- *With a ladle, carefully add sufficient stock to cover the ingredients by 2 cms (⅘ inch). Put the pan over a high heat for 5 minutes and then turn down the heat to minimum and cook for a further 10 minutes until all the stock has been absorbed.*
- *Remove from the heat and leave to rest for 2 minutes.*
- *Turn the pan's contents on to a big platter, as if it were a flan. Serve on individual plates with* baadunseih *(tahina sauce – see p.43 for recipe).*

VARIATIONS

There are in fact few. The only difference is in the arrangement of the layers. However, this is not a regional variation, but one of personal taste.

Nevertheless in the Arabian Gulf and in some regions of the Mediterranean, you will see a gigantic fish in the centre of the platter, surrounded by rice, the whole covered with stock. In this variation, the dish is cooked in the oven for half an hour and then removed. It is served, as in the original recipe, with *baadunseih* (parsley with cream of sesame sauce) – see p.43.

MULUKHIEH
Green leaves

And the startling tale of the octogenarian Emir

The tragi-comedy I'm about to recount all happened just for the sake of a handful of *mulukhieh*. First of all, a diplomatic conflict was almost set in train between an Arab emirate and the Spanish state; secondly, the governor of the said emirate dismissed a general of his own army; and last but by no means least, an order was issued to behead my friend Mustafa, nicknamed Jacobo – for he was unwittingly the cause of the following bizarre story.

Mulukhieh is basically a traditional dish from Egypt and Libya and is well known in the rest of the Arab world. *Mulukhieh* itself is a long-stemmed plant with multiple, opposite, tender, dark-green leaves that vary in size. They give off a peppery acidic smell. Only the leaves are eaten (although in difficult times stems are eaten as well).

My great friend Jacobo is very tiny and not very attractive physically. He has a tough, wrinkled skin like a scouring pad, bulging eyes, and a very small nose above a line of four hairs which form a so-called moustache sketched above an enormous mouth. In fact he had that cartoon face when he was on a tourist trip to Egypt (and still has it). There, in the alleyways of Cairo, he could not resist the temptation to buy a kilo of those splendid, precious leaves of Egyptian *mulukhieh*, and a kilo of halal lamb (lamb that has been killed according to Islamic laws), so that when he returned to Barcelona, where he was living, he could make a dish of *mulukhieh* with lamb.

Jacobo was totally ignorant of the history of *mulukhieh*, whose name came from *mulukieh*, meaning 'royalty' or rather 'the food of kings'. The Egyptian Caliph Hakem bi amr Allah (he who governs through a mandate from Allah) decreed that this plant imported from India was uniquely and exclusively reserved for the use of the *mulak* (kings). So in principle its use was forbidden to the rest of mankind, who called it, sensibly, *mulukhieh*.

That afternoon in the summer of 1986, Jacobo arrived at Barcelona airport and before his turn arrived for luggage inspection by members of the civil guard, two monstrous dogs leapt on his suitcase, barking furiously and continually gnawing at it. The guards immediately called off the dogs, but quite naturally there was a big commotion in the hall. They ordered my friend to put his suitcase on the very long table that served as an inspection counter. Shortly afterwards two policemen came alongside and took the suitcase from him. The two dogs started jostling each other, barking and scratching the case with their paws, extremely put out by the fact that the police were so slow in opening it. An instant after opening it, the two monstrous dogs started fighting a phenomenal battle for ownership of the bag, which they pulled violently from the suitcase, and in which was both the *mulukhieh* and the meat. And while the dogs were devouring what they had obviously been looking for, my friend was taken to a room next to the main hall. Here he shouted over and over again: 'It's *mulukhieh*! It's for eating! It's not hashish!' The police however had never seen those unidentifiable leaves before and were convinced of the dogs' infallibility. All this shouting provoked the intervention of a fat man who had heard Jacobo's pleas and who was in peals of laughter. He and his two companions who were Spanish army officers went into the room to back up the pleas of this poor chap who was screaming in Arabic at the police. The Spanish officers had been told by the fat man that those green leaves were inoffensive, and had a friendly conversation with the police to rid them of their doubts. But they were only finally convinced when they saw the fat man, who was getting slightly annoyed, eat some of the raw *mulukhieh* leaves. From that moment on, everything was explained and a very happy Jacobo was immediately released to his saviour, none other than the general of the pretorian guard of the Emir of one of the most important oil states. The general and the two Spanish army officers were at the airport to co-ordinate and prepare for the visit of the Emir and his retinue.

They did not part company without Jacobo promising to prepare the general a meal of those leaves and make him a thank you visit at the hotel where the whole of the Emir's retinue would be staying. 'Don't worry about the meat,' the general said. ' We bring all our own halal meat.'

The following day, Jacobo decided to fulfil his promise and went to the hotel where the Emir's retinue was occupying the three top floors of the building, so as to avoid any provocative glances from or contact with other hotel guests.

By a very unlucky chance, in the lift, Jacobo hit the wrong button and the lift opened on the floor reserved for the Emir's harem. He had only taken three steps into the lobby on that floor when he spied a woman without her veil, who smiled at him, but when she noticed there was another woman watching them both, she started screaming, 'A man! A man!' hysterically. She was going to make trouble…

The other women told the Emir of the incident, and, totally convinced of his own undisputed power, come what way, he ordered his inseparable general of the guard to bring him the head of the 'rapist intruder'. There was no human way of convincing the octogenarian Emir that in Spain laws other than his own existed. He was not satisfied, he cursed Spain, her government, Barcelona, and his general. He threatened the whole world: 'I won't let them have any oil. I'll cast them into darkness.' Moments later, already out of his mind, the Emir asked for 'the sheik of this accursed country' to be brought to him. The pusillanimous general proceeded to explain to the Emir: *'Tawal allah umrak, sidi'*… 'May Allah give you long life, my lord: there are no sheiks here, but a king, and he cannot come…' While this ridiculous discussion was in progress, the police accompanied Jacobo to the hotel exit and he made himself scarce.

Twenty-four hours later (the 'reasonable' time limit the Emir had ordered for bringing him the head of the 'rapist' – naturally a somewhat unreasonable order), the Emir, followed blindly by his retinue, suddenly brought his visit to an abrupt end and left Spain. The general was relieved of his post. Jacobo *never* held any doubts from then on that the dish was intended exclusively for kings and since then has never eaten or even touched *mulukhieh*, which has been a difficult feat for him, bearing in mind the frequency with which this dish is cooked all over the Arab world.

*

There are two types of *mulukhieh*. The proper one, which is always made with meat, and the other one which is meatless and is known as *mulukhieh kazzebeh* (mock *mulukhieh*). Unfortunately the second is more often made than the first.

MULUKHIEH
Mulukhieh soup

Serves 6

Ingredients

2 kg (about 4 lb) mulukhieh *(with stalks, which will make 500 grams – about 1 lb of leaves.) You can buy tins of mulukhieh leaves, and some- times dried leaves in Arab supermarkets*
500 grams-1 kg (1-2¼ lb) lamb with the bones, or 1 kg (2¼ lb) chicken
1 medium onion very finely chopped
3 cloves garlic, chopped very small
50 grams (2 oz) coriander
1 dessertspoon salt
½ dessertspoon fulful bhar *(see p.206)*
¾ cup samneh
2 tablespoons olive oil
8 large cups water
juice of 1 medium lemon

Method

- *Wash the* mulukhieh *leaves 3 or 4 times and spread them out on a piece of cloth to dry.*
- *Wash the lamb or chicken and cut it into chunks as for a stew. Place the meat in a large saucepan over a moderate heat and gently fry the meat in the oil with the onion for 5 minutes. Add the water, salt and fulful bhar.*
- *Meanwhile, in a frying pan, lightly fry the garlic and coriander with the* samneh *for 2 minutes and then add the* mulukhieh *leaves. Continue frying gently over a moderate heat for a further 15 minutes and then remove the pan from the heat.*

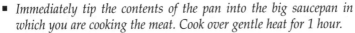

- *Immediately tip the contents of the pan into the big saucepan in which you are cooking the meat. Cook over gentle heat for 1 hour.*
- *When the time is up, turn off the heat, turn out the cooked food on to a large deep plate, and sprinkle with the juice of a lemon.*

SUGGESTION

Mulukhieh is always served with rice as an accompaniment. Usually the amount of rice you want is served and then covered with the cooked *mulukhieh* and the pieces of meat.

VARIATIONS

The only variation, which is traditional and very well known is the one called *mulukhieh nashfe* (dried *mulukhieh*) which is made with the leaves of the same plant that have been dried and chopped so that they can be kept for several months. Its preparation is very simple. Lightly fry the meat in a pan with the spices, salt, onion and garlic. Add 200 grams (7-8 oz) of dried *mulukhieh*, ¾ litre (1⅓ pints) of water and the juice of a medium sized lemon. Cook the pan over a low heat for 1 hour. Withdraw from the heat and serve in bowls, along with a plate of rice.

ورق العنب أو ورق الدوالي

WARAK INAB or WARAK DAWALI
Stuffed vine leaves

...And a Muslim-Christian dispute

I still remember the impassioned and irrational discussions that flared up between my grandmother and the *nasrania* (the Nazarene: which is what Muslims call all Christians. The word encompasses all Christianity's diverse sects: Catholics, Protestants, Armenians, Orthodox – Russian and Greek). The Nazarene and my grandmother, both nonogenarians, had been neighbours all their lives. Both were Palestinians, both widows, both half-deaf and both equally sparkling conversationalists. They would always be sitting opposite one another, with their hunched backs bending them over so much that their heads almost touched. Paradoxically, in spite of all these similarities, they were very antagonistic towards one another and could never agree about anything; not even when it came to the origin of the *dalia* (vine) could they reach a consensus, not even a tiny one. The Nazarene said: ' The Rab [this is how the Arab Christians refer to God, although they also use Allah], when he was angry with Adam, sent an Angel to him to announce his expulsion. The Angel' – the Nazarene infidel went on, now in a cloyingly sweet voice – 'was very gentle with Adam, he was very saddened and tears poured out of him like a stream, and where they fell, a plant appeared whose delicious fruits were eaten by the Angel, who gave Adam a branch of this plant to cultivate in the earth and to feed himself from by drinking its juices'.

I was the messenger boy and carried things for my mother who was, as always, in the kitchen. I carried the vine leaves that both the old women had just finished stuffing, and listened to my grandmother's fulsome rejection of the Nazarene infidel's version of the story. I did not harbour the slightest doubt that my grandmother had not even heard her fellow conversationalist's version at all, so I give you what she said. As stubborn as usual she had to contradict what the Nazarene infidel had said and that was that. 'Your plant', she replied vehemently, 'grew as a result of the irrigation supplied by a ferocious lion, a royal peacock, a monkey and a pig'. From this came the legend that was widespread in all the country districts of the Islamic world, that said that people who drank the juice of the fruits of the vine (grapes) were as ferocious as lions, as conceited as a royal peacock, as devious as monkeys and as dirty as pigs. 'How is it possible for Muslims to drink and eat the fruits of a plant watered by a pig?' the Nazarene asked defiantly. My grandmother defended herself in her own fashion: 'You're an ignorant old woman. Don't you see that for centuries and centuries, since the beginning of Muhammad's message, there are no pigs on the face of the Muslim earth.'

So you see how they were. Seated around the two enormous trays, one of rice and the other full of vine leaves, they debated issues of every possible character. Property deals, marriages, divorces and endless tittle-tattle. On important occasions, such as festival days, families would usually have a great many guests and a large number of women would be needed to prepare the meal. So the hostess would ask friends and neighbours to help, and they would gather for the afternoon, till late at night, stuffing vine leaves, courgettes, etc. The men would be full of trepidation and continually reciting verses from the Koran, when they saw that gathering of women whispering, laughing and discussing things. Apart from the meal, nothing good emerged from this type of gathering. However, paradoxically, the authoritarian and conservative Arab male could not or would not prevent them. He knew, as a good Arab, that everything had to be just so for the following day and it had to be there in plenty. One woman on her own would not have been able to prepare a good banquet, and this would reflect on what sort of host the man was. So the pride of the host was at stake, and this the Arab women knew very well, and thus the husband had very little option but to accept these work parties. I remember my father's set-tos with my mother over just such a party and 'jaw-jaw'. He called the women 'vipers' (a favourite term of his for women), but immediately afterwards, with disguised eagerness, he would extract from my mother all kinds of details about the contents of their female gossip.

In Muslim-Arab farming, the four crops most blessed by Allah are wheat, olives, figs and grapes. Allah takes charge of watering them, since they depend, basically, on rain. The people would eat bread, olives and a few figs and sit on matting under the *arisha* (the arbour of trellised vines). And so they emulated the prophet Nuh (Noah), who was the first viniculturalist in history and who planted the first grapevine in Hebron after the Great Flood.[5] You can see the *arisha* very commonly all over the Muslim-Arab world, set up in fields, orchards, patios, and in the most unlikely corners. The *arisha* is the Arab's air-conditioning during those long unwavering, punishing summers.

When they eat their grapes and roll the vine leaves, the peasants sing the famous popular Arab song:

Among the vines	بـين الـدوالـي
That climb so high	والكرم العالي
How good it is	يا محلى السهرة
To spend the night	والبدر لالي
And see moonlight	جنب العريشة
Around the arisha	نرقص ونغني
We dance and sing	يا محلى العيشة
That is living	وحنا بالجنة
We are in Paradise	

WARAK INAB or WARAK DAWALI
Stuffed vine leaves

Serves 6-7

Ingredients

*500 grams (1 lb 2 oz) small to medium fresh vine leaves (you can buy
preserved ones in Middle Eastern shops)*
500 grams (1 lb 2 oz) ripe tomatoes, chopped
¼ cup (50 grams-2 oz) samneh *or olive oil*
3 medium onions peeled and cut into rings
250 grams (9 oz) lamb or lamb cubes for stewing
1 tablespoon salt

Stuffing

500 grams (1 lb 2 oz) minced meat
½ cup samneh *or olive oil*
200 grams (7 oz) or 1 cup of long grain rice
1 teaspoon fulful bhar *(see p.206)*
1 small spoonful salt
olive oil
1 cup lemon juice

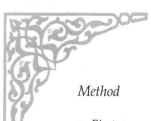

Method

- First, prepare the stuffing. Wash the rice several times, then mix it with the other ingredients (meat, oil or samneh, fulful bhar and salt), then put the mixture on a plate. Set aside.
- In another container, boil 2 litres (3½ pints) of water and blanch the fresh vine leaves in the water for 5-8 minutes. Withdraw from the water and spread them out on large trays.
- In a large saucepan, which will be used for cooking the stuffed vine leaves, first gently fry the pieces of lamb with the butter for 10 minutes. Spread the pieces of tomato and onion over the meat and season. Set aside.
- Using a plate or the table, spread out a vine leaf so that the flat top side rests on the plate or table and the veiny or ridged part faces upwards. Then, cut off the veins and stems.
- Put a tablespoonful of stuffing in the centre of each leaf, fold over the sides, then roll the leaf towards its point. Repeat the same process with all the leaves.
- Pack the little rolls in the cooking pot in orderly rows, and always with the point of the leaf on the bottom side; this detail is essential to stop the rolls unrolling during cooking and spilling their contents, in other words turning the whole thing into a disaster. Once you have positioned all the rolls in the pot, sprinkle them with a spoonful of olive oil and a cup of lemon juice.
- Cover the rolls with an inverted plate to press them down and stop them moving, and then cover everything with hot water. When the water has boiled, turn down the heat, put the lid on the saucepan and leave for 30 minutes. When the water has been absorbed, cover again with hot water and leave it on a low heat until the second lot of water has been absorbed.
- Now, withdraw the pot from the heat and leave to rest for 5 minutes.
- Place the rolls on a large platter or in a large dish or on a tray. They are eaten just as they are, or moistened with a little creamy Arab yogurt.

VARIATIONS

Many varieties of this dish exist and almost all are made this same way. The only difference that one can see is based on the variation in contents.

One of the variations is *malfuf* (stuffed cabbage leaves), a dish which is also very popular. It is prepared in the same way as given in the instructions above.

MAHASHI
Stuffed vegetables

Town versus village

They say that Arabs will stuff (with rice, meat, spices etc.) any vegetable that can be hollowed out. That includes aubergines, courgettes, cucumbers, carrots, swedes, peppers. These dishes are laborious to prepare but they are worth the effort. Although the ingredients and the method are basically the same for all these vegetables, the flavour, be in no doubt, is totally different. The best known stuffed vegetables are the aubergines and the courgettes.

بيتنجان محشي

BETINJAN MAHSHI
Stuffed aubergines

The Arabic name for aubergines, *betinjan*, presumably comes from *baid-al-jan*, 'the devil's eggs', or rather 'the devil has laid eggs'. Their attribution to the devil is because of their blackish colour.

This is a dish as widespread as stuffed courgettes. They are prepared the same way and have the same characteristics. On many occasions both dishes are prepared at the same time, but in different cooking pots so that their tastes are distinct. It would not be surprising if they all went into the same pot: stuffed courgettes, stuffed aubergines along with stuffed vine leaves. This mixture of stuffed vegetables has a unique aroma and flavour, which has no equivalent in any other sort of cooked food, and is usually found in country places and in more traditional family settings in the Near East, as opposed to the big towns. The *medani* (people from the medina or city) pull grim faces and make fun of the very generous, vernacular style of cooking in country districts. It is precisely because of this that people from the *medina* are harshly criticised and accused of meanness. The offering of individual dishes to the guests – although the host does not put one in front of himself – limits freedom and is a restraining influence on the guest's enjoyment. In the villages, the host will set a big table with enormous copper trays, full to overflowing with stuffed aubergines, courgettes, vine leaves, that form a small mountain,which is covered with numerous enormous bits of lamb; and they eat, with no plates or cutlery.

Very often the host simply spends his time offering drinks (water), and replenishing the tray of food every time its massive bulk begins to diminish. I confess, in spite of my status as a *medani*, that eating and handling those stuffed vegetables with your own fingers confers on them a peculiar delicacy that is not there if you use a plate and a knife and fork. Muhammad recommends eating with your fingers and sucking them when you have finished. In my childhood, I remember the envy I felt towards the children of the el Fahmawi family, our neighbours. They were peasants who had abandoned their village in Palestine and relocated to Nablus as refugees. Their children never lost their self-possession as they swarmed up the stairs of the small building where we lived, and in the alleyways and on the flat roofs, they bit with real pleasure into their stuffed vegetables. For me, it was a hymn to liberty and unconcern that they could play while they were eating; in contrast, my brothers and I, the townies, were obliged to stop our games to go and eat inside our house. That hiatus seemed to me like an eternity, it never seemed to end. I would protest bitterly that I wanted an aubergine in my hand and to play on the street like my friends and neighbours. But my parents would only answer me contemptuously with, 'We're not *falahs* [peasants].'

Dear reader, if on any occasion you find yourself as a guest in the house of a peasant, don't let it worry you, they will take your status as an *afranji* (foreigner) into consideration and immediately provide you with a plate and cutlery. It would be a most agreeable gesture if you were to refuse this offer and throw yourself into the feast like the rest, with your hands. Don't worry about anyone having dirty hands, because it's a tradition to offer – before and after eating – soap and water to wash your hands. Don't forget this last procedure, and do not do as Don Quixote did, who was ignorant of this Arab custom: instead of his hands, he doused his beard in the washbasin offered by a servant. Curiously this custom which is very widespread in Arab countries is totally ignored in some regions. In the south of Saudi Arabia, Bedouin deliberately don't wash their hands after a good banquet. The smell that their hands give off, after not washing, is an indicator of a good feast and this adds a certain cachet to someone, especially if the smell is of a *jedi* (a kid). This custom was noted in the 1950s and related by my uncle, General Innab, chief of staff in the Jordanian army, on his visits to southern Arabia. Nevertheless, today thanks to oil in that region, the Bedouin have changed the barometers of boastfulness. Instead of feeling pride from the smell of roast kid on their hands, it's now the Rolex watches incrusted with diamonds on their wrists.

I return to the main theme of this section. The aubergine in all probability originated in India and was spread by the Arabs through their conquests. Now we believe that the stuffed aubergine dish is of genuine Persian origin. Stuffed vegetables were the favourite food of the great Arab gourmet, Ibrahim el Mahdi, author of the well known *Kitah eltabikh (Book of Cookery)*, probably the first of its kind in the Arab world. He was the little brother of the Caliph of Baghdad, the great Harun el Rashid. Ibrahim rebelled against his nephew, the Caliph Maamun, son of Harun, and he was defeated and imprisoned, but after a few years was pardoned. Prince Ibrahim dedicated the rest of his life to gastronomy and the hideaway in which he lived with his concubine Badi is well known. She was a great and clever cook. It was at this time that he wrote a large part of his famous cookery book.

The ingredients and the method follow exactly the same steps for stuffed courgettes.

كوسا محشي

KUSA MAHSHI
Stuffed courgettes

I burst out laughing the first time I saw European courgettes of such monstrous proportions, curved, hard, and, as if that were not enough, green. 'What can these courgettes be used for, and how would it be possible to hollow them out and stuff them?' I asked darkly of my shopping companion, a Syrian addicted to broad beans who explained to me that Europeans prepared courgettes in all sorts of ways, except stuffed. My mother, however, was more ingenuous when she visited southern Europe at the end of the 1970s. Her disillusioned comment was: 'How is it possible that people in the south of Europe, especially the Spanish, say they're like us if they've never heard of *kusa mahshi?'*

The great majority of Arab students and tourists who visited Spain in the 1970s did so through reading advertisements and job announcements in the Arab press and posters on walls in Spanish embassies in Arab countries. These ads showed reasonable prices, bulls, flamenco, beautiful girls, and the greatest of all inducements, the magic phrases: 'Spain of the Umayyads', 'Moorish Spain' etc. 'Yes, yes, very Arab and they don't even have small *kusa* (courgettes),' my mother continued her lament. 'Where those damned *kafara* (north Americans) live, the long and the short of it is, they have everything and we have nothing whatever to do with them.'

It was only a couple of years later that we had a wonderful surprise. On one of my visits to little markets, in a small village on the Spanish-French Mediterranean coast, where at weekends the countrywomen display their produce for sale in enormous baskets, I found those small, yearned-for courgettes, fine, straight, fresh, and their authentic yellow colour thrilled me. I bought the whole huge basketful. The countrywoman looked perplexed when I told her that my great purchase was made neither for a restaurant nor for a record-breaking, giant omelette, but simply to entertain a few fellow countrymen living in Barcelona and Madrid. That Catalan peasant woman, with her weatherbeaten, goose-pimply, scaly skin who had probably never achieved such a huge sale in her life before simply murmured: 'The Moors have been thin on the ground till now. Fancy them making such a fuss over courgettes.'

KUSA MAHSHI
Stuffed baby courgettes

Serves 4-6

Ingredients

2 kg (4½ lb) baby courgettes, straight and slender
1 kg (2¼ lb) raw ripe tomatoes
500 grams (1 lb 2 oz) finely minced lamb or veal
200 grams (7 oz) long grain rice
1 medium onion
2 dessertspoons salt
50 grams (2 oz) samneh
1 teaspoon fulful bhar *(see p.206)*
3-4 cloves garlic, peeled
juice of ½ lemon

Method

- *Wash the courgettes and cut off the tail end. Reserve these to use as caps for the courgettes later. Hollow out the inside. Be careful. If you break one, pierce it, or one begins to crack, throw it away immediately as it will be useless, and furthermore if it bursts during the cooking, it will unbalance the genuine flavour of the dish.*
- *Wash the rice several times and drain. Mix with the meat and add one of the spoonfuls of salt, the spices and half the butter. This mixture is the* mahshi, *the stuffing for the baby courgettes.*
- *You need to fill each of the hollowed-out courgettes three quarters full. This detail is very important, because when you cook them, the rice will expand, so there must be sufficient room to avoid the courgette bursting.*
- *Cap the courgettes with the ends or 'tails' you kept back. Shake the courgette so that the stuffing is evenly spread.*
- *Prepare another mixture with half the tomatoes and onion, peeled and cut into pieces, the butter and salt. When you've made this mixture, it is to go in the bottom of a large saucepan, which should not be too deep. This will form the first layer of the dish.*

97

- *Start placing the courgettes immediately over this layer. Pack them in side by side in an orderly way.*
- *Prepare a sauce with the remaining tomatoes. Grate them and mix them with 2 cups of water, the minced garlic and lemon juice. Pour the sauce into the saucepan so that the courgettes are completely covered.*
- *Put the saucepan over a high heat for 10 minutes and then reduce it to minimum. Leave to cook for a further hour.*
- *Once you have turned off the heat, the dish is served on a big platter or a tray, covered with its own succulent juice and the slices of tomato and onion.*

SUGGESTIONS

Stuffed courgettes are served immediately, shared out on individual plates. As with aubergines, don't be surprised if on some occasions stuffed courgettes are presented on a big communal dish, with no individual cutlery. Treat it as a sign of informality and a desire to share everything. Sometimes you may feel ill at ease when there are no napkins on the table and, if there are, as often is the case in the big cities, listen, wiping your hands on napkins does not excuse you from washing them in soap and water at the end of the meal.

VARIATION

There is one variation that is widespread in the big cities and particularly in privileged groups with sophisticated cooking habits, and if I may say so, I shall be so bold as to admit that this version is totally superior to the original.

Preparing this version is very easy. Once you have finished cooking in the way I have already explained, remove the courgettes from any of the sauce. In a saucepan oiled with a spoonful of oil and one of *samneh* (clarified butter), and seasoned with a pinch of salt, brown the courgettes without scorching the skin. Since we are in refined circles, they should be served on individual plates, a maximum of 2-3 per person, garnished with slices of lemon and fresh mint leaves on the side. Without a doubt the combination of colours gives this dish an indisputable refinement and contrasts with the local Arab dishes known for their copiousness and abundance.

شيخ المحاشي

SHEIJ EL MAHASHI
The sheik of stuffed vegetables

Sheij is an adjective that is used to venerate people, and in the Arabian Gulf countries it is used as a title to denote nobility. Among the Bedouin, only the chief of their tribe can employ this title. But nowadays in the rest of the Arab world, this title confers no superior status. Calling this dish a sheik is a figure of speech that signifies we should venerate it, the reason being that the stuffing, apart from a little onion, is made exclusively from meat. As we have already seen, the presence of meat in any dish symbolises prestige and nobility.

The ancient chronicles written at the time of the Ottoman Empire tell the story of a Sultan who fell into a faint, so bedazzled was he by the magic and delicacy of a dish made with aubergines stuffed with greens, and served by virgin slaves 'of moonlike beauty'. We shall never know exactly whether the Ottoman caliph suffered this misfortune because of the exquisite sobriety of the food, as the chroniclers and *aficionados* of this dish imply, or from the abundance of oil it contained, as the palace doctors implied, or, most probably, from the extravagant beauty of the slave girls, as was said by malicious tongues. Whatever the reason, the Turks would name this dish, *Imam bayildi* – 'The Sultan fainted' or 'The delicacy of the Imam'.

Curiously, although I am not a sultan, this dish was once directly responsible for my fainting too. This happened when my father gave me a resounding smack in the face for refusing to eat it, without even tasting it. 'Allah is great!' my enraged father exclaimed. 'How is it possible that this good-for-nothing dares to turn his nose up at the *Sheij el mahashi* – the lord of stuffed vegetables?'

Little by little, the Arabs of the Near East have substituted the original stuffing of greens with meat and a little onion. These ingredients, of course, elevate the status of the dish, and that is why it is called what it is.

However, for me at that time, just smelling and seeing the slices of half fried onion in the stuffing was more than enough to turn my stomach. So, out came my father's hand and gave me a black eye.

My mother had a cure for the fainting fit that my father's clout had brought on. She gave me what was called the *Tasset el ruub*. It was a magic bowl, in which there was a little water, enough to regain the consciousness of whoever had fainted, whatever the cause. This little bowl was made of copper and inscribed inside and out with numerous *suras* (verses from the Koran) along with drawings of the cosmos. Arabs believe that many miracle cures can be effected just through drinking a little water from this bowl. For example, it's used as an antidote for all types of fright, fevers, snake bites, rabies, and in my case, my poor appetite or total lack of it.

'Now you'll eat, now you'll eat,' my mother said to me, attempting to pacify my father's anger. 'Look, it's already working. The child's drinking water from the *tasset el ruub,*' she insisted. My mother put a portion of the Sheik of Stuffed Vegetables on my plate and carried me to another room, where, with awesome speed she devoured the food herself, and in spite of my opposition, wiped my lips with some of the sauce. We immediately returned to the dining room with the empty plate. My father was incredulous and could not stop glancing at the magic bowl, made in Mecca and brought from there, which had endowed it with absolute infallibility. To avoid any fresh arguments, my mother never cooked this dish again at home.

We now need to move on thirty years – yes, thirty years exactly – to find me once again with this hated dish. It was in Turkey in 1993. Without realising it, I accepted the waiter's recommendation to try the Turks' traditional dish *par excellence*, the famous *Imam bayildi*. Imagine my surprise when I saw that the plate set before me held something extremely similar to the one I had hated throughout my childhood and which had been completely erased from my memory. At first I eyed it cautiously, then as a compromise I tasted it and, finally and incredibly, I ate it with great pleasure. So you see it took thirty years for the *tasset el ruub* to perform its miracle and turn my most hated dish into what is without a doubt my favourite.

This dish is traditional in Mediterranean countries and in each one there are minor differences in its preparation. I've tried many variations and I personally opt for the Jordanian-Palestinian one, which is prepared as follows:

SHEIJ AL MAHASHI
The sheik of stuffed vegetables

Serves 4

Ingredients

4 medium aubergines
250 grams (9 oz) minced meat
2 medium onions, chopped and sliced very small
200 grams (7 oz) chopped tomato sauce (tinned, in a jar, or fresh)
1 teaspoon fulful bhar *(see p.206)*
1 dessertspoon salt
1 dessertspoon freshly chopped parsley
1 dessertspoon freshly chopped coriander
1 tablespoon samneh
olive oil for frying
2 cups meat stock (not pork), mixed with
1 cup of chopped tomato sauce

Garnish

Pine kernels

Method

- Cut the tails or ends off the aubergine, peel them lengthwise leaving some narrow strip of skin, and finally cut them lengthwise in two, and hollow them out (not totally) leaving a thickness of not less than ½ cm (⅕ inch).
- Soak the aubergines in water for 15 minutes.
- While they're soaking, prepare the stuffing. In a frying pan over a moderate heat, lightly fry the onions with the butter and when they become transparent, add the meat, salt, spices, parsley and coriander. When the meat is cooked, add the tomato sauce and continue cooking for a further 5 minutes. Turn off the heat and put the stuffing to one side.

- Take the aubergines out of the water and fry them, hollow side down, in a shallow frying pan, with a little oil (not more than ½ cm [⅕ inch] deep) and over a low heat. Take them out of the frying pan when they are lightly golden brown, especially the ends (this detail is very important, because the part nearest the ends is usually tougher than the rest and therefore requires more cooking). A word of advice. When the aubergines are frying, make sure you cook the ends for 2-3 minutes extra, and then remove them from the pan.
- Arrange the aubergines in a row, hollow side up, on a baking dish.
- Immediately, start filling them with the stuffing, using a spoon. Garnish them on top with about 7 pine kernels. Once they've all been prepared and garnished with the pine kernels, pour the stock into the baking dish and put it into a pre-heated oven at about 180°-200°C (350°-400°F, Gas 4-6) for 30-40 minutes, or until three quarters of the stock has been absorbed.
- Take the dish out of the oven and place it on the table as it is. It is always eaten hot and accompanied by white rice.

VARIATIONS

FETTET MAKDUS BETINJAN
(Lebanon)

No one knows why the Lebanese call this dish *makdus*. Throughout the Arab world, including Lebanon, *makdus* and *mjalal* refer to vegetables preserved in salt. On the other hand, the word *makdus* means 'pressed together' or 'pressed', or may be one thing pressed on top of the other. As you will have seen, the original dish was neither pressed nor preserved. In this variation, many *fettet* or small slices of Arab bread (that have been toasted) are placed under the aubergines before they are cooked in a big shallow saucepan, and not in the oven. In Eastern Europe, Persia and India, etc., there are many different versions of this dish.

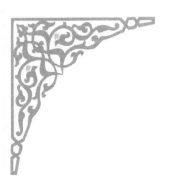

HARIRA
Ramadan soup

This is the soup *par excellence* of the North African Arabs of the Maghreb, which, along with couscous, is the most famous dish in that region, though it is rarely found in the Middle East. *Harira* is known as Ramadan soup, because although it's consumed throughout the year and especially in the cold season, during the sacred month of Ramadan all the faithful break their fast almost daily with *harira*. It's no exaggeration to say that at the moment of *Iftar* (breaking the fast) at sunset, the whole region of the Maghreb is redolent with the smell of *harira*. In contrast, in the Near East, one or two hours before *Iftar*, the air is agreeably scented with the smells of rosewater and orange blossom, ingredients found in all the local confectionery and pastries, especially *katayef*.

After consuming the soup, the Maghrebi, to my great surprise, have a glass of milk, some dates and some of them also have pastries, then they take a breath and go on to eat their main course, such as *couscous, tahina* or *bosif* (swordfish with almonds) etc. In the Muslim-Arab world, the nights of Ramadan stretch from *Iftar* till dawn. After finishing the huge meal, people carry on nibbling fancy or luxury foods, intent on cramming themselves full so they can withstand the test of the fast the following day. True believers censure the extravagance practised by the majority, such behaviour nullifying the effect of the true message of Ramadan – one of humility and austerity.

There are several variations of *harira: Bidaui* and Marrakeshi or classical. Both are made primarily with chickpeas, lentils and meat, as the basic ingredients, and secondly with many different kinds of greens and vegetables. Then, as we know, every cook will brand it with her own special touch.

MARRAKESHI or CLASSICAL HARIRA
Ramadan soup

Serves 4

Ingredients

100 grams (4 oz) lentils
100 grams (4 oz) lamb or veal cut into pieces, and some bone
1 medium onion, peeled and cut into small pieces
500 grams (1 lb) tomatoes
1 dessertspoon salt
½ dessertspoon pepper
1 pinch saffron
a good bunch of parsley, chopped (100 grams [4 oz]) and fresh coriander, chopped (20 grams [just under 1 oz])
2 tablespoons flour
1 tablespoon virgin olive oil
1½ litres (just over 2½ pints) water

Method

- *Heat the water in a large saucepan and add the lamb meat, the bones, lentils, onion, pepper, saffron and 1 spoonful of salt. Put the lid on the saucepan and cook over a moderate heat for 30 minutes.*
- *Meanwhile skin the tomatoes and chop them up, and lightly fry them in a pan with the oil for 10 minutes over a low heat. Once fried, put the tomato into the main saucepan. Stir from time to time.*

- *At the end of 10 minutes remove the lid from the saucepan and from that moment on stir continuously for 5 more minutes, until the cooked mixture acquires a consistency which is neither thick nor thin.*
- *Serve hot.*

VARIATIONS

Some cooks add a little rice, which has been cooked separately. Others add a splash of lemon juice. It is served with dates or on its own, and the same dish is frequently cooked with chickpeas instead of lentils. In the Libyan-Tunisian desert, this same dish is made with both lentils and chickpeas together.

الكسكس

AL-CUZCUS, AL-KUSKUS
Couscous

...And the guide who got lost

When we first heard the name of this dish, we couldn't stop laughing. It was in 1966 in the holy city of Al-Kuds (Jerusalem) in Palestine. One of the Algerian students said it. The Algerians had just obtained their independence from 'Mother France' and had come to the Near East to take courses in 'Arabisation'. The Algerian was explaining how this dish was prepared. Naturally, two times out of three he used the word 'cuscús'. We were only adolescents then and were always laughing. The poor Algerian didn't know that in Near Eastern colloquial Arabic *cus* means 'cunt', and he was only making an even greater ass of himself by not just mentioning one solitary cunt, but two at a time.

The word *couscous*, according to most anthropologists and linguists, is of Berber origin from the Atlas Mountains in the Maghreb.[6] It is little known in the rest of the Arab world. It refers to the sound the steam makes, when the fine grains of a special semolina are cooked through the *kiskas* (a sort of finely meshed strainer or steamer that is placed in the top of the saucepan, in which the greens and meat are being cooked). Other authors maintain that the origin of the word is Sudanese Arabic and derives from the Arabic word *cascasa*, which means the division and grinding of something, in this case, wheat.

The history of this dish goes back hundreds of years: for example, it was known during the rule of the el Nasrid dynasty (in the thirteenth to fifteenth centuries) in Granada, but was unknown during the remaining era of the *ta'ifas* – the independent kingdoms of Muslim Spain in the eleventh and twelfth centuries.

In 1967 the Israelis invaded the rest of Palestine, including eastern Jerusalem. The Algerians were immediately repatriated. They had not had time to learn Arabic, nor to teach us how to prepare couscous either. So, after that, I had had no chance to taste that dish again, nor did I even hear it mentioned again until 1972. It was in the summer of that year and I was accompanying a group of European and South American students on a trip to Morocco. That country was at that time *the* place where hippies from all over the world tended to gravitate. Our destination was Ketama, a Moroccan locality totally unknown to me. However, such was not the case for my travelling companions, who knew perfectly well why they were going to Ketama: 'Everything's cheap, including *kif*[7] my companions kept telling me. They asked me to help them by interpreting for them, although it soon became very clear that I was useless. And everything that had, in principle, been seen as an advantage in taking an Arab as a guide turned into serious inconvenience. I couldn't even help when we disembarked in Tangier – the Moroccan police made my entry into the country difficult *because* I was an Arab. Paradoxically, Europeans and foreigners in general have a much easier ride entering and visiting Arab countries. But the regimes of these countries invent a thousand and one bureaucratic impediments to make entry for their fellow

Arabs from fellow Arab countries difficult. That is the shocking reality.

My companions who were certainly worldly wise and expert in such messy situations came to a successful agreement with the police officer – in French of course – on the appropriate amount of *bakshish* for my entry into the country.

Right after this, our poor car, a dilapidated Seat 600, made a supreme effort and crossed Tangier in five minutes in a south-easterly direction. We arrived, without planning to, in Xauen, a small, typically Moorish village, made up of little white houses whose balconies and shutters were decked with hundreds of white and red geraniums. The village was surrounded by hills in the shape of horns – hence its name – Chef Chauen – and in that very place, among those hills, the bloody battles waged by the Riffian leader Abdel Karim had been fought against the Spanish and French colonialists.

In one of the little streets of white plastered houses in that peaceful village, we stopped at a sort of restaurant bar which had three tables indoors and several more on the romantically decaying patio further inside. Its white walls were invaded by dozens of little flowerpots overflowing with masses of neglected geraniums of every hue. In the centre of this patio grew a solitary, tall, majestic palm tree from whose upper part sprouted an infinite number of long leaves and enormous racemes of dates. In the shadow of the palm we rested and ate some dates that were lying, unpicked, on the ground.

Palm trees were blessed by the Koran and by the Prophet Muhammad who in his flight from Mecca across the desert came across only a few palm trees. He rested in their shade and fed himself with their fruit.

The local customers in the bar were constantly giving us looks and making gestures to us, mostly intended for my companions. They wanted to sell us *kif*. My companions urged me to get into conversation with them. I couldn't understand anything clearly; the Moroccans kept talking to me about *kif*, but I was completely ignorant of what it was at that time – I had never heard the word before. My lack of knowledge of the subject completely threw the Moroccans and they lost their trust in us, paradoxically just when I began speaking to them in Arabic. They couldn't understand my Arabic (the way it was spoken in the Middle East) and suspected that I was an agent of the police secret service, and for the rest of the time chose to have nothing to do with us. At that precise moment, in a state of complete frustration, my job as interpreter came to an end and remained so for the rest of the trip. Very quickly we ate the delicious kebab, took tea and immediately continued our journey towards Ketama, our original destination.

We drove down a narrow track between dense woods of pine and cedar until we reached the Riff town. My friends immediately began to hallucinate. 'Smell, smell!' they were saying to one another. 'Can you smell marihuana?' one whispered, and then and on a sudden impulse uttered some mellifluous howls in the style of the King of Soul, James Brown. In fact, all I could smell was the stench of the thousands and thousands of dollops of dung from the thousands of goats and sheep which accompanied us all the way and on both sides of the street. Here in Ketama everyone claimed to be Riffians, a signal of pride and synonymous with insubmission and arrogance. But in fact we encountered locals much more humble and likeable than the legend proclaimed. When we told them we came from Spain we were entertained far more royally than the other European tourists. They offered us tea, dates, cakes…I was sincerely amazed by the special fondness the Riffians had for the Spanish, in view of all the barbarities that the Spaniards had perpetrated against them during the colonial period.

At little cost, we lodged in private homes. During the three days we stayed in Ketama, they didn't allow us a single free moment from eating, drinking and smoking. Inside their homes, they made us feel as though we were starving Biafrans, but white-washed, although they were enchanted with our excessive and strange appetites. The one who was happiest and simultaneously most dis-couraged about our unexpected bulimia was our landlady. Every time she saw us she invoked the name of Allah and his prophet over and over again, imploring us to relieve our ravenous hunger at her house. The more gluttonous we were, the more dishes were offered us. I believe that in those three days we must have eaten practically everything in the Moroccan culinary repertoire and in the Maghreb in general: *harira* (soup), *chakchouka* (a kind of sainfoin with eggs), *tahina* (garnished with meat), sheep's brains, a thou-sand kinds of salad, brochettes of fish, *meshwi* (lamb roast-ed over hot coals), many different kinds of pastries and dozens of cups of tea. Of all these there was one dish that was never missing from the table, and I remembered eating it for the first time when the Algerian student made it for us in Jerusalem. It was *couscous*.

I shall never forget those three days in Ketama. In that short space of time and in the same lodgings, I saw every-thing from circumcision, the slaughtering of animals, a wedding, even a divorce... And nor shall I forget the two following days in which the whole group of us were admit-ted into hospital in Oran (Algeria) with indigestion.

The variety of ingredients is what most distinguishes one type of *couscous* from another. The most famous are those that use lamb or chicken with seven different greens (*bidaui* or *kedra*). Generally it's made with swede, courgette, broad beans, tomato, pumpkin, raisins and honey. Without a doubt, *couscous* with chicken or lamb and the seven greens is the most widespread. Sometimes they don't include the seven greens, but six or five, depending on what is available at that particular time of year. Also, there's no obligation to include this precise quantity.

When she was preparing *couscous*, my landlady in Ketama gave me her recipe. She did it by eye and with no measurements to follow. 'Tell your mother,' she said to me, 'to add a handful of chickpeas like this, or a little bit of pumpkin. Then tell her you add the butter like this.'

As you can see, the landlady never thought or believed that it was I, and not my mother, who wanted to learn how to make that particular dish. As I reminded her of this detail, she gave me a smile and said, 'Oh, really?' 'Yes,' I replied firmly. She paused slightly, glanced doubtfully towards her husband who was outside the kitchen awaiting one of his clients. Then with an air of resignation she carried on. 'Ah, and before I forget,' she said, 'tell your mother that the onion…'

AL-KUSKUS
Couscous

Ingredients

200 grams (7 oz) soaked chickpeas (soaked 4-5 hours in water)
1 onion finely chopped
⅓ cup of olive oil

1 aubergine cut into fingers
3-4 carrots, peeled and cut into long pieces
2 large potatoes cut into fingers
2 cloves garlic
4-5 skinned tomatoes
100 grams (4 oz) pumpkin
2-3 baby courgettes
1 handful coriander, chopped very finely
1 handful parsley, chopped very finely
½ small cauliflower
100 grams (4 oz) green kidney beans
½ dessertspoon pepper
1 dessertspoon ginger
100 grams (4 oz) butter
1 pinch saffron
1 small piece of cinnamon stick or a pinch of ground cinnamon
2 small spoons of salt
500 grams (1 lb 2 oz) couscous (made from processed semolina, now easy to find in supermarkets or in Middle Eastern shops)
1 kg (2¼ lb) of lamb, veal or chicken, cut into stew-size pieces

Method

It would be wonderful to be able to use the traditional utensils to cook couscous. As I am aware of the difficulty of finding them in markets outside the Maghreb and France, I shall use kitchen utensils that are universal; for example, you can substitute a fine-meshed strainer or a vegetable steamer for the traditional cuscusera.

- In a large saucepan over a moderate heat, lightly fry the meat or chicken in the oil and butter. After 5 minutes, add the salt, parsley, onion, garlic and all the spices. Gently fry all the contents for 5 more minutes.
- Fill ¾ of the saucepan with water and when it boils, mix in all the greens, vegetables and the chickpeas.
- While they are cooking, wash the couscous, drain it and season it with a tablespoonful of oil and a pinch of salt.

- *Put it in the strainer or steamer over the saucepan to cook it in the steam from the broth. At the end of 10-15 minutes, remove the couscous and put it into another receptacle, preferably an earthenware one, which is big and shallow, so that you can spread it out well.*
- *Add another glass of water, a spoonful of oil, and a pinch of salt. Mix it all again and put it back into the fine-meshed strainer or steamer. You must repeat this stage three times.*
- *I recommend that you always keep it on a moderate heat. Finish off the cooking when the meat and the contents of the saucepan are well cooked.*
- *Serve the couscous on individual plates covered with the meat, greens and vegetables. Pour the broth on top of all this (to the eater's taste).*

Before finishing this chapter, I should like to say to all those who're inexperienced at making couscous, among whom I include myself, that you probably won't find any difference between the innumerable types of *couscous*. Nevertheless, according to those who know, no *couscous* tastes the same as another, although they may be made in the same way and with the same ingredients. There's always a hint of distinctiveness, be it regional or individual.

VARIATIONS

I shall follow the principles of this book faithfully, or maybe make things easier and encourage the reader to put these recipes into practice. But in any case…if I began listing all the versions of *couscous* there are, I would undoubtedly have to use several chapters to do this. This is due to the distinctive characteristics of the different regions that make up the huge area of the Maghreb. In some villages of the Middle East a dish very like *couscous* is made, which is known as *maftul*.

JUDRUAAT BI LAHMEH
Meat stews

It wouldn't be practical to include all the stews that are known in the Arab world in this book, because a huge number of variations exist.

In Arab gastronomy stews differ slightly from those made in Mediterranean countries in southern Europe. As a general rule, we can say that the stews made in the Eastern Mediterranean (and by extension in all the countries of the Near East) differ from those made in Western Mediterranean countries in the following ways:

1. Only on rare occasions do the peoples of the Eastern Mediterranean include more than one type of vegetable or greens in the same stew; also if we're talking of, for example, green kidney bean stew, only kidney beans and meat will be in the pot. In the Western Mediterranean (and in Britain too), on the other hand, it is more usual to mix various greens and vegetables. *Tajin* in North African Maghrebi and Spanish stews vouch for this.

2. In the Eastern Mediterranean (including non-Arab countries) the stews are almost always served with an accompaniment of white or pilaf rice to give more consistency to the menu; however, in the Western Mediterranean, it's rare to be offered rice as an accompaniment to a stew.

3. The number of stews that exist in the Western Mediterranean is much smaller than in the Eastern Mediterranean. There, the variety of stews they've succeeded in creating is inexhaustible. We can mention a few, as for example, carrot stew, cauliflower stew, potato stew, kidney bean stew, okra stew, chickpea stew, swede stew, aubergine stew, and so on.

ANNABIT BI LAHMEH MAA RUZZ
Cauliflower stew with rice

I've chosen this dish to represent stews in order to vindicate this vegetable, which as we know enjoys little sympathy, and an almost outright rejection by most people, particularly the young.

ANNABIT BI LAHMEH MAA RUZZ
Cauliflower stew with rice

Serves 4

Ingredients

1 kg (2¼ lb) cauliflower cut vertically through the stalk into pieces
1 small onion
1 medium garlic, peeled and chopped very finely, mixed with a pinch of freshly chopped parsley
1 kg (2¼ lb) of lamb, veal or chicken, cut into stew-size pieces. I recommend spring chicken.
oil for frying
1 teaspoon fulful bhar *(see p.206)*
a pinch of cumin
3 cups of water
2 dessertspoons samneh
1 dessertspoon olive oil
salt

Method

- *In a frying pan over moderate heat, gently fry the meat or the chicken with the onion, salt and* fulful bhar *for 5 minutes.*
- *Put the fried meat in a baking dish and heat it in the oven until it is totally cooked. Alternatively you can cook the meat completely in the same frying pan.*
- *Pour 3 cups of water into a medium sized saucepan and place it over a high heat. When the water is hot, add the meat or the chicken, put the lid on and continue cooking for 10 more minutes.*
- *Meanwhile on another ring over a medium heat, heat the oil in a deep frying pan and gently fry the cauliflower until it has browned completely. Immediately add the fried cauliflower to the saucepan.*
- *In a small frying pan, put the two spoonfuls of butter and olive oil and, on a gentle heat, lighty fry the garlic and the parsley.*
- *Next, add to the saucepan all the contents of the frying pan and turn down the heat right away.*
- *Serve in a large deep dish and sprinkle with a pinch of cumin. Serve hot and always with white rice as an accompaniment.*

MUHAMMAR BATATA
Potato stew

To make this dish, use potatoes instead of cauliflower. The rest of the ingredients are the same as those used in the previous recipe. So, then, peel the potatoes, cut them up into bite size pieces and wash them. Then follow the same steps for cooking the previous dish.

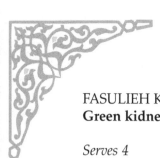

FASULIEH KHADRA BI LAHMEH
Green kidney bean stew

Serves 4

Ingredients

500 grams (1 lb 2 oz) fresh green beans, tailed, strings removed, and cut into 1cm (⅖ inch) pieces
1 kg (2¼ lb) lamb, veal or chicken, cut into stewing size pieces
1 medium sized onion, skinned and chopped very small
1 garlic peeled and chopped very finely
½ cup of olive oil
1 × 250 gram (9 oz) tin of chopped tomato
1 dessertspoon salt
1 dessertspoon lemon juice
1 teaspoon fulful bhar *(see p.206)*
3 cups water
a pinch of cumin or cinnamon

Method

- *In a casserole over medium heat, heat the oil and add the meat or chicken, the onion, garlic, beans, spices and salt. Gently fry them for 10 minutes. While they are frying, stir all the contents of the casserole.*
- *Next, add the water, the chopped tomato and lemon juice.*
- *Put the lid on, turn the heat down and continue cooking for a further hour.*
- *Serve hot in a large deep dish and sprinkle the cumin or cinnamon or both on top. It is eaten, like the previous dishes, with white rice made the Arab way (see p.60).*

لحمة مع بيض

LAHMEH MAA BEID
Minced meat with egg

Food of the Elect

This is a very easy dish to prepare and at the same time a
bit of a 'luxury' for most Arabs. It's eaten by the well-off
and the spoilt, people with poor appetites, high civil servants, business people who're short of time. We're talking
here of a dish that is very high in calories and also very
expensive (in the 1950s and 1960s, meat and eggs were
enormously expensive for the majority of Arabs). Nowadays, although these items are not so expensive as then, the
situation still prevails.

I remember that my brothers and I, as adolescents, sometimes pretended we were ill in order to be given this food.

In Arab countries, the tradition is that the best food is
usually reserved for the menfolk. They are the ones who
work, and consequently they are the backbone of the family and household, so the family backbone must be kept
strong. I still remember this everyday scene: the whole of
my family would be gathered round the pot of *mjadarah*
(rice and lentils), except for my elder brother, who worked
in Jerusalem, for whom my mother often prepared this
'exceptional' dish. After the first mouthful, my brother
would be infuriated and cursing one saint after another
because of our envious looks, which took away all the

pleasure of eating it. So he would then share it out among the smallest of us and stomp out into the street, fuming. My mother would bless him from the window and at the same time warn him to 'keep away from the sons of sin' (the Communists). And my brother would do exactly the opposite: he joined them, and helped organise the popular revolts of the 1950s.

Later when it came round to exam times, our chances of tasting the delights of this dish increased. If we wanted to go on to take a more advanced course, then very high marks were required, and students needed an excess of energy to achieve this. So their mothers would serve them large, appetising meals. And to save time, mothers would frequently carry their meal to the terraced roofs of their homes – the favourite place for students in towns to study. Students in villages, on the other hand, preferred the roadsides where there were very few passers-by and very little traffic. The confined space inside homes belonging to people of modest means, and who generally had a great many children, added to the lack of libraries, meant that thousands and thousands of students taking exams had little choice but to go out into the streets or on to the roof tops. Out there in the street with people passing by, there would be many a timid, shy look exchanged between both sexes, and often heart-rending emotional entanglements would ensue, only to meet tragic ends.

Today, there is no city or village in the Arab world, however small, which does not have its own street known colloquially as the 'Street of the lovers'.

But to return to our dish: this is served on its own in the Arab world, and in a small quantity, and is usually made just for one.

LAHMEH MAA BEID
Minced meat with egg

Serves 1

Ingredients

100 grams (4 oz) minced meat
1 large onion chopped very finely
1 egg
1 tablespoon virgin olive oil
1 tablespoon samneh
1 small spoon salt
1 small spoon fulful bhar *(see p.206)*

Method

- *Lightly fry the onion over a moderate heat in a frying pan with the butter and oil. When it is transparent, add the minced meat, season and sprinkle with the* fulful bhar. *Stir the whole mixture over the heat.*
- *Once the meat is cooked to your own taste (rare, well-cooked etc.) add the white and yolk of the egg and continue stirring the new mixture for 2-3 minutes, until the egg is cooked.*
- *Serve on a plate and eat it with bread. If the bread is Arab, so much the better, because you can mould this type of bread into a scoop.*

As I've said, this is a dish just for one. If you want to prepare it for a great number of diners, clearly you're rich! Just multiply the ingredients by the number of people.

VARIATIONS

Various versions of this exist; the flashiest, *Lahmeh math-uneh maa beid* was made for us by a guitarist at the Nasim el Andalusi school[8] (moved from Andalusia) in Algeria, with the same ingredients, but in this version the meat was made into meat balls and the egg fried separately. It was eaten with a little bread, a meatball and a bit of egg. It has the same flavour as *Lahmeh maa beid*.

كفتة، كباب وشوارما

KAFTA or KIFTE, KEBAB and SHAWERMAH
Meat on a skewer

How is it that there are so many open-air stalls selling brochettes of *kebab* (meat) and fish, the length and breadth of the Arab world? The simple answer is primarily one of economics. Most of these stalls don't pay taxes, or rates, so running costs are very low, and as a consequence the prices they charge for their brochettes are very reasonable. In the second place, Arabs generally don't have much liking for restaurants and are inclined to avoid them, if only because if you're seen eating in a public restaurant, people will pigeonhole you as *maktuh* (someone who has no family and hasn't got their life together). From this, you can guess that Arabs don't think of these stalls as restaurants. Eating at one of these stalls is thought of as having little seriousness, a passing fancy. People are often just passing and are lured unexpectedly by the smell, they pause by a stall, eat what they have on offer and then walk on.

Someone will ask, what do travellers do if there are no restaurants? In the Arab world, the traveller will always meet some family, however far away he may be, or a friend or direct or indirect acquaintance who will see that he's looked after. If this weren't the case, it would be as insulting for the traveller as it would be for the rest, and both parties would accuse each other of having little *assl* (noble roots).

I shall digress a little. Twenty-five years ago, a distant cousin of mine, almost certainly a millionaire, visited me in Spain. At the time I was still a student. I could not give him lodgings in my one very small room, rented from a land-lady on the usual conditions, which went as follows: 'No visitors allowed. No cooking allowed'. Naturally, I thought it would be a good idea to take him to a restaurant. Since then, a quarter of a century has passed, and my cousin, his family and some of his acquaintances continue, always, to reproach me, not just me, but by extension my parents and brothers, for this 'abominable offence' against the decency and tradition of *assl*.

On the trip I took with my friends, all the way through Morocco, Algeria and Tunisia, apart from the big towns, all along the difficult roads that link the sands of the Sahara, the oases and the villages of trogladyte houses, we would stop every now and then and eat delicious brochettes of *kebab* and *meshwi* until we were full to bursting. For so much food we paid laughable prices. For less than the value of a French franc, they served us with brochettes, bread, water, some pastries or dates, and mint tea. On various occasions, they treated us to brochettes and wouldn't take any payment – they simply asked for the blessing of Allah in exchange, 'Allah, who when all is said and done', the stallholders said, 'is the most generous'.

In the countries of the Arab Orient, the same also happens although, there, *falafel* and *shawermah* are more common than the *kebab*.

What is *shawermah*, this famous wonderful snack that, along with *falafel*, is invading Europe and the entire world? It is not thought of as a dish, nor as food that's eaten at home, and least of all as restaurant food, but rather as frivolous, street food. It is not prepared for anyone on their own nor for small groups of people, but for huge numbers.

When *shawermah* first began to spread across the Middle East, it was exclusively these stalls that sold it; today, given the great increase in this food, some restaurants, even though they may be quite high class, will, fearless of criticism or of losing their culinary reputation, install a huge *sij* (metal skewer) in some corner or other, on which are speared slices of meat, to form the popular core shape of the *shawermah*. Even so, the *shawermah* should not be given up as a street meal. In the Western world, it's categorised as fast food. It is reasonably priced, and for that we see thousands of couples, particularly the young, but older people as well, eating these snacks before or after their evening out.

No one knows the origin of this meat roast for certain. Turks, Iranians, and some of the countries of the Caucasus all argue their claim for it. I believe that the food in itself is no great invention, if it were not for the spices and sauces that people in these Eastern countries add to the roast meat. It's well known that all these peoples included roast meat in their diet, and still continue to do so, but obviously not all prepare it in the same way.

KAFTA BROCHETTES
The ingredients are the same as for *Kafta* (which is explained on p.132). While the meat for the *kafta* (as in the main recipe) is spread on a tray and always cooked in the oven, in this version, the meat is shaped in the form of fingers or cigars and cooked on skewers over a brazier, in the oven or fried in oil.

SHAWERMAH

This food is not suitable for preparing at home, because of the complicated machinery that is needed, and because, as we said at the beginning of this book, our main objective, apart from helping readers learn a little about the Arab culture that surrounds cooking, is to encourage you to prepare and enjoy these dishes in an uncomplicated way. So, because of this difficulty, I shall merely list the ingredients and give you some idea of its preparation.

After the lamb meat has been treated properly, it is cut up into large slices, cleaned, seasoned (according to the individual cook or region) and the slices laid together and threaded over the large metal skewer, one on top of the other, to form a huge trunk And finally this is placed upright on top of specially made revolving machinery to roast. The rest is easy. Once cooked, the first layers of meat closest to the heat are sliced off with a very sharp knife and put inside Arab bread. Then many different types of sauces and salads are added.

As is known, the Ottomans held a large part of the Arab world under their dominion for almost four centuries. This important fact had a great influence, as we've seen, on Arab gastronomy. Without making any unfavourable comparisons, it is a known fact that the population of northern Iraq (mostly Kurd) and of northern Syria, because of their proximity to the Turks (great and insuperable masters of the art of preparing *Shawermah)* learned the art of this type of roasting from them. And so, they have unquestionably become the best in the Arab world.

KEBAB

Most Arabs call this *sij kebab*, the Turks *shish kebab*, and the Greeks *souvlakia* (although this can also refer to meat cooked on the bone sometimes). Despite the fact that they will deny this, basically they all prepare it in the same way, with a few insignificant variations. Each country proclaims itself the best. In reality, everything depends on the ingredients; for example, suckling lamb or kid is more delicious than mature lamb or veal. The same can be said of the spices and sauces that accompany it, the fire (grill or griddle pan), the cook…and most important, it depends on the consumer's palate.

KEBAB
Meat brochette

Serves 4-5

Ingredients

1 kg (2¼ lb) leg of lamb (boned), sinews and fat removed, cubed
2 green or red peppers, or one of each, cut into squares
500 grams (1 lb 2 oz) medium-sized onions cut into quarters (optional)
500 grams (1 lb 2 oz) medium-sized raw tomatoes, cut into quarters

Marinade

1 cup olive oil
1 dessertspoon salt
1 dessertspoon white vinegar
1 teaspoon milled black pepper, or better still, the classic Arab fulful bhar *(see p.206)*
1 bay leaf
1 garlic clove, mashed
½ cup lemon juice

Method

- *Prepare the marinade and soak the meat in it for 2-4 hours.*
- *After you've finished marinading, thread on to the bamboo or metal skewers (which I prefer), alternately a piece of meat, a piece of onion, a piece of tomato, a piece of pepper. Or if you wish you can thread a piece of meat, then onion, then meat, then tomato, then meat, then pepper, and finally meat again. I would advise you not to fill the whole of the brochette so that you can handle it more easily when you come to grill it. Place all the brochettes on a gridiron or greased griddle pan over medium heat. Roast for 10-15 minutes (according to whatever criteria the cook and the consumer have). You should baste them while cooking with the marinade.*
- *Serve hot, with Arab bread and an infinity of accompaniments, sauces, salads...*

My preference is for a salsa of yogurt and cucumber as a natural accompaniment to this type of roast. But some Western countries claim that there are two basic inconveniences in its preparation. First the scarcity or absence of creamy sheep's yogurt, and secondly few enjoy the good fortune of having the small sweet oriental cucumber with no seeds. I have already given an alternative to this authentic salsa (see my chapter on Dips and Salads).

KAFTA
Oven-baked minced meat

...And the vilified left hand

The *kafta* that is made today is in no way equal, in taste or aroma, to that of years gone by, of the 1950s, 1960s and 1970s. Modernity (Ah! modernity, simultaneoulsy convenient and irksome, and the undoubted destroyer of anything genuine) has completely annihilated every natural thing required in the preparation of an authentic *kafta*. I'm referring to proper grazing for sheep, their husbandry, the method of slaughter, then of preserving the meat, the freshness of the spices and vegetables etc. However, what has been the greatest cause of the genuine *kafta*'s disappearance is the almost total – there are just a few still working – disappearance of the primitive traditional oven. The one shaped like a natural cave and hand built, fuelled simply on almond shells and olive stones. These leftovers were placed in a hollow channel on the left side of the oven, then lit. In the right part of the oven was the cemented paved area or paving stone on which was placed the *gift* of Allah (bread), *kafta*, pastries etc. for cooking. As we've already seen, the brazier, or hell or sin is always situated on the left, while 'gifts' are situated on the right. In Arab tradition – and in others as well – all good is always associated with the right hand side. For example, you greet others with your right hand, you enter and leave houses, mosques and cemeteries with your right foot; you venerate your elders by kissing their right hand; you sow the ground with your right hand etc. Only by fulfilling this total ritual, even when making *kafta*, shall you enter into the thousand miracles *Inshalah* (if Allah so wishes).

When the oven-man used to remove the tray of *kafta* from the oven, he would pause for a few moments to admire his handiwork, and exclaim, as was the custom, *'Allah u akbar!'* (Allah is great). This exclamation is not just a war cry, as people in the West will tell you in their tendentious, deprecating manner, but it has significance in various other ways. In this case, for example, the oven-man is valuing his own work, but by explaining it this way, recognises Allah as the most perfect, and that He is the Supreme One, and none other than He can perform perfect deeds. So the Muslim, when he stands marvelling at something, be it food, a film, a song, works of architecture, a horse, a beautiful woman, will traditionally make this instant exclamation. The oven-man was, however, implying at the same time that his own work was irreproachable; in other words, he should be well rewarded and without argument. From the time when I was very small, I was given the responsibility of carrying the tray of *kafta* from my house to the oven and back again. So, after the meat had been roasted in the oven, I would say to the oven-man, 'My father says to tell you that you should take a morsel' (as remuneration for his work). He, as was the custom, had his big knife ready and would cut off a piece, murmuring in agreement: 'According to the teachings sent by Allah and his Prophet, that is to say, the Just One'. With those words, the oven-man justified his reward. Immediately he covered the tray with another made of raffia or wickerwork, or with a piece of cloth or simply a piece of paper. The practice of covering food in Arab countries is very widespread. Its basic objective is to keep away the evil eye of envious people and the gaze of beggars. If you run into a beggar and he manages to get to know what the food is in the packet you're carrying, you can be sure that if you pass him by without offering him part of the food, that meal will be indigestible. For that reason, my mother always advised me not to answer any beggar if he asked me about the contents of what I was carrying. Frequently my mother disconcerted me by emptying our icebox of the bits of food it contained and sharing it among the beggars who called discreetly at our door, while on other occasions she forbade me even to answer them. 'But *Yamma* [Mama in Arabic], Allah, in the Koran, says that you should respond to beggars with friendship, even though they'll give you nothing.' She, like most mothers in situations of scarcity, was a good caretaker of the family budget and would answer me elusively and laconically: 'Do as I say, and when you're bigger, you'll understand.'

With a few rags, the oven-man would make a little cushion, which I would place on my head, and on top of this protective bundle, he would place the tray of *kafta*. Then he would put a small piece of cloth in each of my hands so that I could keep the hot tray in place. 'Go with Allah.' Thus would I be sent off by the oven-man. 'Home, eh.' As I started off, the tray would burn like a brazier, but minutes afterwards, on the way back home, it would cool down. From then onwards I would reach out with my right hand – naturally, always the right hand – towards the contents of the tray and with my fingers tear off a tiny piece or two. At home, many mouths were waiting to be fed: ten brothers and sisters, parents, my grandmother, my aunt and some others too. How frequent it was and how probable it was that the small ones were always given the worst bits, and I, forestalling them somewhat, assured my portion on the way. It was so easy to blame the selfish oven-man for the pieces that had disappeared. Not knowing the truth, my mother was limited to cursing the 'greediness of the *far-ran* – the oven-man', quite unjustly. However, to protest or claim back from the oven-man or from anyone else for such a motive was considered a sign of unpardonable meanness in Arab tradition. That happy virtue of ours released me from an inevitable row.

As I said before, genuine ovens are almost totally extinct. All the houses now have their own insipid electric ovens. If public ovens have disappeared, the same has happened to the children. Now they no longer swarm through the alleyways of the Middle East – happy children who played marbles and other children's games, as they waited for the *kafta* or bread to be cooked. Today, while their *kafta* is cooking in the 'modern' ovens at home, the majority of our 'born-to-have' children are sitting down, staring unblinkingly at the television adventures of Mazinger Z and all the Rambos.

KAFTA
Oven-cooked minced meat

Serves 4-5

Ingredients

¾-1 kg (1½-2¼ lb) of very finely minced meat
2 large onions, chopped very small, or minced with the meat
500 grams (1 lb 2 oz) of raw tomatoes, sliced no more than 1 cm thick
200 grams (7 oz) tomato purée or chopped tomato
2 teaspoons fulful bhar *(see p.206)*
2 teaspoons salt
200 grams (7 oz) fresh parsley, chopped very finely: never use dried
a sprig of fresh coriander

500 grams (1 lb 2 oz) potatoes, peeled and cut into rounds ½ cm thick
1 tablespoon clarified butter
2 tablespoons virgin olive oil
50 grams (2 oz) pine kernels
juice of 1 large lemon

Method

- Grease the oven tray with butter. In the same tray, knead the meat with the parsley, coriander, onion, a spoonful of salt, a teaspoon of spices and the oil. This well mixed 'dough' is then flattened and stretched into a rectangular shape in the tray with the kaf (the palm of the hand), so that it is no more than 1 cm (⅓ inch) thick. You have to leave a border of 1 cm in width free between the meat and the edge of the tray.
- Put the tray into an 'integrated' oven, one which gives off the same heat top and bottom, at 250°C (450°F, Gas 8) for 20 minutes.
- While you are cooking the meat, fry the potato slices in oil.
- Prepare a raw tomato sauce. Put the tomato purée or grated raw tomato into a container and add the lemon juice and the remaining spoonfuls of salt and spices. Stir all the contents thoroughly for 2 minutes. You can substitute this sauce with a tin of chopped tomatoes. My recommendation would be a mixture of both, the raw and the tinned, in equal parts.
- Take the tray from the oven and cover the meat with the fried potatoes. Over the potatoes lay the slices of raw tomato and on top of the three layers (meat, potato, tomato) pour over the tomato sauce, covering the layer of meat. To garnish, add some pine kernels on top of the tomato slices.
- Put the tray back in the oven and heat the top part to 200°C (400°F, Gas 6) for 15-20 minutes, just enough time to brown the pine kernels and the slices of raw tomato.
- Take out the tray from the oven and place it in the centre of the table, so that the guests can see it newly made. After it has been admired by all present, serve on individual plates. The guests and the father of the house are always served first and take the best bits.
- It is always eaten with bread, and in some regions it is accompanied with a little rice.

VARIATIONS

The most important and most interesting variation is *Kafta bi tahina* (Minced meat with sesame sauce).

TAHINA
Sesame sauce

Ingredients

½ cup tahina
1 cup water
juice of ½ lemon
½ teaspoon salt

Method

- *In an earthenware bowl, mix the* tahina *with the water, lemon juice and salt.*
- *Beat all the ingredients until you obtain a sauce which should be more liquid than thick and slightly acidic.*
- *The sauce can be prepared to suit individual tastes.*

The principal ingredient of *kafta*, minced meat, is prepared and cooked in the same way as for the oven-cooked *kafta*, but instead of adding potatoes and tomatoes, you add this particular sauce. Sesame sauce, cooked in the oven, has a unique flavour and is without equal among all the sauces known.

Because this version is easy to prepare, this type of *kafta* does not have the same respectability as the main kind of *kafta*, so if you serve *kafta bi tahina* it is a sign of lack of willingness on the part of the wife to go to any trouble for the guest (the wife usually being the cook, as you know).

I won't be out of place if I say that one of the causes of clearly perceived cracks in the structure of Arab society is in the change of cooking habits among its members. They can be seen occurring each time with greater frequency. Arab women are reading easy recipes that originate in Western cooking, or they pick up the telephone with amazing nonchalance and order a take-away pizza, little interested in their husband's desperate looks. However, there is not much one can do about this other than to resign oneself to modern ways.

As we said before, preparing this dish is simple. Once the meat is cooked in the oven, you take out the tray from the oven, add the sauce and put it back into the oven for a further 5 minutes.

Egyptian *kafta* is similar to the original, but the Egyptians add fried aubergines and many more hot spices.

الأوزي

AL UZI
Stuffed lamb

...And the wily Bedouin girl

My uncle, General Innab, told me that the best *uzi* ever made was the one he tasted in the 1940s in the *jaima* (tent) of some Bedouin nomads of Iraqi origin in the Jordanian desert of Wadi Rum or Rem, near the Saudi and Iraqi border. It was in this beautiful, spectacular desert, with its night skies studded with stars, that Lawrence of Arabia, the English spy, had his adventures.

'And how did you come to be in the desert, *Khaloh*[9] [uncle]?'

He burst into loud guffaws that finished in a fit of coughing, a frequent habit of his, and it perturbed none of his listeners who were packed together around a brazier, which eased the chill of that cold wintry night. The children were waiting for the General to start telling a story about some skirmish or other. For some mysterious reason, the adults wanted him to shut up, and this provoked protests from the youngest, who insisted on knowing everything.

'But will you promise me that you won't do what your idiotic cousin Karim did?' All, except the adults, answered 'yes', not having a clue as to what cousin Karim had done.

'What I must do for certain – and better late than never – is to warn you of the tricks women get up to, for there are some women who'd swindle Satan himself. Allah, the Supreme One, said: "Nothing equals a woman's guile."' And he went on: 'Your cousin Karim was a commercial traveller. He travelled from place to place with his mules, carrying fabric and perfume, and buying and selling his merchandise.'

'One morning he ran headlong into a black silhouette, mounted on a donkey. The silhouette was clothed in a long black dress that covered her whole body from head to toe. All you could see were two big black, provocative eyes shining out, but that was enough to drive your cousin Karim mad. He was completely besotted and followed her little caravan with its fantasy of bewitching eyes from Petra to Wadi Rum. There he caught up with the 'silhouette's' tribe, made a few bad sales of his merchandise and

General Innab (first on right) with King Hussein

returned to Nablus (in Palestine) deliriously in love. He had to marry this Bedouin girl, come what may.'

While my uncle was telling us this and laughing, the adults tried to hide the fact they were laughing too and shook their heads to left and to right, in protest against my uncle, who, since the children were so persistent, continued with his tale. 'We told your cousin it wasn't possible, because they were Bedouin and we were from the city. We were at cross-purposes with them in almost everything, our traditions, religion, law, and so on.' (The Bedouin are generally Muslim, but not strict.) 'All our arguments were useless – we simply couldn't convince him. He was totally blind.'

Seeking the hand of this 'silhouette' from her parents was difficult enough in itself. The first and inevitable question the Bedouin asked foreigners (and Karim was a foreigner, as far as they were concerned) was: ' And how did you come to know this girl?' And if the way he had gone about it was considered indecent, there would be an instant rattling of sabres and a rattling off of shotguns. To tackle this problem head on, he sought out my uncle at the military range. Through his work, my uncle had been in Jordan, Palestine, Syria... My uncle pretended to the Bedouin family that he had seen the girl on some occasion and begged for her hand for his nephew. The word of a military man was seen as sacrosanct and they immediately believed him. After various courtesy visits, the Bedouin family consented and accepted the proposal without opposition, something that greatly astonished my uncle. Another strange thing was when they were entertaining my uncle, all the members of the Bedouin family were presented to him and it was noticeable – though he didn't pay much attention to it at the time – that all the women went with their faces uncovered, except for the girl being courted. All she revealed were her enormous eyes made up with traditional kohl.

My uncle returned to Nablus, bringing all his observations with him and also the list of conditions and demands of the bride price. The women in Karim's family wailed to the heavens: no way were they going to accept this liaison, and began cursing the Bedouin girl. 'She didn't even offer coffee[10] – it must have been to hide the fact she was a *zaara* (dwarf). And she only kept her face covered because she was hideous.' The real reason the women gave these opinions of her was because it meant certain loss of a marriageable male from their own family, and this in turn could mean a new *kasera* (spinster) in the extended family. The men too showed little enthusiasm for Karim's betrothal to a Bedouin girl, because it would drain their financial resources, since the Bedouin girl did not come from their own family. Furthermore the Bedouin girl's family would demand a disproportionately high bride price for her, because the Bedouin would be losing a marriageable woman from their own household. That meant that a man from their own tribe would be left without a wife, and, because of this tipping of the scales caused by the foreigner Karim, it would now mean that he would have to seek a woman from another clan, and such a move would cost him a higher bride price. Karim and his family would be to blame and he would have to pay for her. What a mess!

One after another all the women refused to take part in the female committee who normally were sent to represent the prospective bridegroom's family in order to inspect the bride. This inspection consisted of making the would-be bride laugh so that they could see the state of her teeth, stroking her hair to make sure the girl wasn't wearing a wig, and embracing her effusively in order to feel the size of her breasts, to be certain of her ability to breast-feed.

Being unable to sway the women's decision not to collaborate in such a fundamental step in Arab marriage ritual, and faced with his cousin Karim's determination, my uncle went on to list the demands of the bride price:

- 10 camels for the father
- 1 camel for the mother to compensate for the time she spent suckling her daughter
- 10 *liras* for the cousins of the betrothed, to compensate for the loss of 'matrimonial primacy' with the young girl (a privilege of her cousins who take precedence over men from elsewhere). Should the intended groom not obey this rule (i.e. pay up), he would be considered *madsus* (an intruder).
- 1 kid for each young male member of the bride's clan, for the same reason as above. This act is known as *Shat el Shahab* (the young men's kid). Some of the richest Bedouin compensate the young men with pistols or rifles.
- 10 *liras* as compensation for the uncles of the bride; this payment is known as *balsa*, and compensates for the loss of a niece, who, in principle, could have been destined for a cousin, or perhaps, their own brother.
- 1 *lira* for the servant who leads the bride's camel, when she abandons her paternal home.
- *Jahsh el Kiláb* (the donkey for the dogs). You have to offer compensation right down to the dogs. The bridegroom must offer a donkey, either whole or in pieces, for the dogs, as a thank you for custody of the girl during her childhood.

Despite occasionally losing track, my uncle pressed on animatedly with his story. 'Your cousin and our whole family joined forces to pay the bride price and the costs of the wedding feast with its special dishes. At nightfall the wedding was consummated in a special *jaimat shaar* (a tent made from goatskins) which was prepared for the event. On the following day we travelled back from Wadi Rem towards Palestine on camelback. On the way, your totally embarrassed cousin announced to us that Fatima (for that was the bride's name) was defective because no human being was allowed to see her face. She had refused, calling on her rigid Bedouin tradition, which in principle opposed unveiling, even to a husband.'

Four months later and when Fatima announced her pregnancy (which was essential to please and keep her husband), my uncle went on, 'I didn't have the slightest doubt that her announcement was a reason and a good occasion to unveil in front of Karim. This she did, and when Karim saw his sphinx of a wife he fainted. She was totally *fatssa* (flat-nosed).' We all burst into peals of laughter. 'Her nose,' my uncle said, 'was so flat that Karim's mother was flabbergasted – she couldn't stop examining "this thing", totally forgetting her son lay stretched out on the floor. A few hours later, the whole district knew of the scandalous and comic affair. From then on Karim's family was known laughingly as "the *fattsa*'s family". Karim didn't waste much time in gathering up his wife and emigrating with her to New York, where he made a great fortune.'

'And when will our rich cousin come back?' all of us asked, astonished. 'Never,' was my uncle's sad reply. Twenty-five years after the unveiling of the nose, the multimillionaire Karim and his wife, now with her nose cosmetically reconstructed, and now both US citizens, visited Nablus as tourists, a city which had taken in many Palestinian refugees like Karim's parents. The multimillionaire asked the taxi-driver where the Innab family, his own family, lived. The taxi-driver answered him by asking, 'Do you mean the *fattsa*'s family?' 'Son of a bitch,' Karim stuttered. He ordered the taxi-driver to do an about-turn and negotiated with him to take them immediately to the Damia bridge (the Jordanian frontier). From there they went to Amman and from there they returned to New York, never to return to the Near East. All of us listening were overcome with sadness, especially the children, for not having had the opportunity of getting to know a multimillionaire in the family, and thus losing the chance of receiving a *hadeya* (present).

'So then, so it seems you don't want to hear anything about the wonderful *uzi* we ate that year?' My uncle wanted to dissipate the cloud of frustration that covered our illusions. 'Well then, as I said in the beginning, it was the best *uzi* I've ever eaten. It was unsurpassable! No Arab or Turk could better it. Those illiterate Bedouin slaughtered the kids, according to Muslim ritual [they utter the name of Allah, turn towards Mecca and then slit the animal's throat] and hung them by their feet for two hours to drain away all the blood. At the end of an hour, a Bedouin put a kind of tube in the kid's anus, blew in air and inflated the little animal, then took his very sharp dagger from his belt and in the blink of an eye skinned the little animal in one whole piece. Then, through a single slit in the belly, he totally disembowelled it, cleaned it with water and lemon once and then again; then he smeared it with a mixure of salt, garlic, cumin and melted butter. The next step was to hang it by its feet for 4-5 hours so that the meat could "rest". The Bedouin say that this way the meat is tender and mellow. Later, two women came and began to stuff the kid with the *hachue* [stuffing] and sewed up the slit in the animal's belly with strong thread. They covered the animal with an enormous Bedouin bread like a huge pancake and on top of the bread placed some rags. The kid was ranged on a baking dish and placed in a strange primitive *tapun* (pit oven).[11] Every half an hour they poured two glasses of water into the dish. The cooking lasted for five hours.

'Ah,' the general exclaimed, 'I shall never eat such tender meat like that again.'

It is undoubtedly lamb, that is thought of as the most venerated ingredient in the whole of the Arab world. The greatest honour that a guest can be offered is to offer him the *zabiha* (slaughter of a sheep), and prepare it in the form of *uzi* or *guzi* in the Near East, or in the form of *mashui* (roast without stuffing) in the north of Africa.

The *zabiha* (the slaughtered and cooked animal) has to be served with the entire head, a sign that the meat is fresh and has been slaughtered in the guest's honour. Don't think that they offer *zabiha*s for just any occasion. No! It has to be for a very important event, such as *zabiha Ramadan* to celebrate the end of Ramadan, the Muslim month of fasting, *zabiha el Haj* to celebrate the culmination of the arduous pilgrimage to Mecca, *zabiha el dar*, to demonstrate happiness and give thanks to Allah for being able to build your own house (after the roof has been put on, they slaughter a sheep, sprinkling its blood over the front of the house – this way the house is blessed and ghosts will be frightened off. *Zabiha*s are also performed for the birth of a son, to mark the end of ones studies, or on the release of political prisoners (never criminals), etc. The meat from the *zabiha*, with the exception of that for the guest, is all shared amongst the poor, or, as a minimum, a third of it is. It's well known that this gesture (the sacrificial slaughter) is meant to emulate the *sidna* Ibrahim (the patriarch Abraham).

AL UZI
Stuffed lamb

Serves 20

Ingredients

11-12 kg (24-26 lb) lamb, which has been bled when killed (this last detail is very important for the special flavour it imparts)

several lemons
2 kg (4½ lb) minced meat
7 cups white long-grain rice (Basmati is the best)
9 large cups of hot water
200 grams (7 oz) raw white almonds
200 grams (7 oz) pine kernels
200 grams (7 oz) raw pistachios, shelled (optional: in Syria and Turkey, this ingredient is basic)
5 tablespoons salt
6 tablespoons cinnamon
6 tablespoons black pepper
6 tablespoons mixed cumin and turmeric
6 tablespoons ground cardamom
3-4 dessertspoons ground saffron
1 dessertspoon ground nutmeg
2 large cups samneh

Method

First and foremost, we recommend a lot of patience!

Stuffing

- *Pour a cup of butter into a frying pan of medium size and depth. Over a medium heat, brown the almonds and at the end of 2 minutes add the pine kernels and lower the heat. Once they are both browned, remove the pine kernels and the almonds and put them to one side.*
- *Brown the pistachios for 5 minutes over a gentle heat and add them to the pine kernels and almonds. Drain off all the butter.*
- *Place the minced meat in a big saucepan (of 4-5 kg [8-10 lb] capacity). Add 3 tablespoons salt, a tablespoon each of ground saffron, cinnamon, black pepper, cumin, turmeric, cardomom and a pinch of nutmeg. Lightly fry over a low heat, stirring continually. At the end of 10 minutes, add the rice (well rinsed and drained 4-5 times) and the 9 cups of hot water. Proceed to cook, over a low heat for half an hour, continually stirring with a wooden spoon. Withdraw it from the heat, and add the browned nuts. Stir again, so that you finish up with a homogenous mixture. This is the* hashue *(stuffing).*

The lamb

- *Wash the lamb carcase well, remove the entrails and leave it to dry out. Then rub it with lemon inside and out.*
- *Use half of the remaining spices to make a mixture with which to smear or sprinkle the inside of the carcase, and use the other half to do the same with the outside.*
- *Place the stuffing inside the carcase through the small slit, which you then sew up after completely filling the cavity, especially any crannies. Then position the front and back legs close to the carcase and tie them in to reduce the overall size of the lamb and place it in a very very large saucepan or cauldron. Add 8 cups of water and 2 tablespoons of salt, cover the pot properly and wrap the lid in a cloth. Put the pot on the fire, or whatever cooking apparatus you're using, at first over a high heat, until it begins to boil. Then reduce the heat and leave it like this for 5 hours. Every 30 minutes you have to take a quick look inside the saucepan to check the evaporation of the water. Add small quantities of water however often it is necessary to avoid total evaporation.*
- *Remove the lamb from the saucepan and place it in the oven to brown, for 15-30 minutes.*

This is the most modern and most practical version in modern cities in the Arab world. The second version is also modern and can be done indoors, although you omit the huge saucepan. After you've stuffed the lamb, prick it all over (not very deeply) with a fork and put it straight into the oven. The cooking will take 6-8 hours, though clearly this will depend on the type of oven. The method you follow is almost the same as for the first version. You cover the lamb with tinfoil and place it on a baking dish. In the bottom of the dish you put 4-6 cups of water with a tablespoonful of salt (which has been melted in hot water). Afterwards you go on adding water in the same small quantities, every time the salty water has evaporated. At the end of 5-6 hours, you can test the meat. Before taking it out of the oven, you must check that the meat from the lamb melts in your mouth, without you being forced to chew it. When it reaches this point, turn off the oven, take out the oven dish and serve the lamb from that.

Undoubtedly, the most 'genuine' way, and the most difficult nowadays is the Bedouin one.

VARIATIONS

UZI AL SHAMI
Damascus stuffed lamb

This is the only variation known as an authentic dish. It is only cooked this way in the capital of Syria; in the rest of the country and in the rest of the Arab world, it is prepared the way we have just explained.

The Damascus version is as follows:

You make the stuffing in a similar way and with similar ingredients to the one already described, but then it is moulded into orange-sized balls and with an outer layer, curiously, of pastry. No lamb, nothing else, and improperly also called *uzi*.

YAY MAHSHI
Stuffed chicken

The drama of the feast

There are many notable feasts in the Muslim calendar. The two best known and most celebrated are the *eid el saghir* (the feast of the last day of Ramadan) and the *eid el addha* (the sacrificial lamb feast, or the feast that represents the end of the pilgrimage to Mecca). Muslims, each according to what they can afford, plus some more, celebrate the two sacred events with a lunch based on stuffed or roast lamb, kid or chicken. The most splendid (which are not always those cooked by the richest families) opt for the lamb. Whether this latter option is laudable or no, sooner or later it creates a bad atmosphere, in which children play a leading role. Let me explain. Arab children, like children the world over, think of animals as their friends. But in Islamic culture, dogs[12] are forbidden because of their lack of self-control when it comes to hygiene, and cats are anarchic and insubmissive; in other words, they cannot be relied on. And so all the children are full of eager anticipation as these feast days approach, and beg their parents to buy a live little kid or a baby lamb ahead of time. Through the days before the ritual slaughter of the little animal, it becomes an inseparable friend of the children in the family, who treat it in an incredible way. They carry it to pasture,

147

wash it, play, talk and sleep with the little kid and also carry it, clandestinely, to school with them. What happens on the day appointed for the ritual slaughter? What happens is what everybody has been expecting to happen. All the children form a human shield between the animal and its unprepared butcher; scuffles and fights break out, but finally the adults get their way, and in the end there will be several very miserable days for the smallest children after their little animal has had its throat slit.

Why do parents accede to the children's pleas to buy a kid or a baby lamb? some readers may ask. The answer is simple: a month before the feast day the children start begging and they do not stop making a nuisance of themselves until the parents buy the little animal. What is absolutely certain is that no child who has lived with the little animal will ever eat its meat. I remember clearly as a boy, my brothers' and my own emphatic refusal to eat the meat that our neighbours gave us as a present from the lamb that was cared for by all the children in the block before it was ritually slaughtered. To avoid such a situation and for other reasons, my father never bought a live lamb, nor do I recall ever having eaten stuffed lamb, until only five years ago. My father always opted for chickens.

YAY MAHSHI
Stuffed chicken

Serves 4

Ingredients

1 × 2kg (4½ lb) chicken
100 grams (4 oz) minced meat
½ onion, peeled and chopped very finely

100 grams (4 oz) Basmati or other long grain rice
50 grams (2 oz) pine kernels and raw white almonds
4 dessertspoons samneh
2 dessertspoons salt
1 dessertspoon fulful bhar *(see p.206)*
a pinch of ground cardamom, saffron and nutmeg
1 lemon

Method

- *If it has not already been done, remove the neck, feet etc. of the chicken, remove the intestines and lightly singe the bird.*
- *Wash the outside of the carcase well, and wipe the inside with lemon*
- *Mix all the spices together. With half the mixture, sprinkle the inside and outside of the bird.*

Stuffing

- *In a frying pan over a moderate heat, put 4 dessertspoons of samneh and brown the pine kernels and almonds. Add the onion, then the minced meat and gently fry.*
- *Then, add the rice and the remaining spices.*
- *Stir all the mixture for 5 minutes, then withdraw it from the heat.*
- *Stuff the chicken with the contents of the frying pan and wrap it in tinfoil.*
- *Cook the chicken on an oven tray at 170°C (325°F, Gas 3) for 3 hours.*
- *Every 20 minutes you need to check that the chicken is not drying out, and when necessary pour in a cup of boiling water in which a teaspoon of salt has been dissolved.*
- *Minutes before finishing the cooking, remove the tinfoil to brown the chicken.*

ZAGHALIL or HAMAM MAHSHI
Stuffed pigeon

Assault on the pigeons of Genoa

Throughout the Muslim-Arab world this is a highly prized dish, for the Prophet Muhammad blessed this bird and had his own pigeoncote. So it's difficult to meet a Muslim who has not at some time in his life had a pigeoncote on the roof of his house.

I have not eaten pigeon for thirty years. The last occasion I did so was horrible. On my first trip to Europe, our ship anchored in the port of Genoa. Another travelling companion who was Egyptian and myself exploited the few hours we were docked to have a look round the outskirts of the port. We reached a square where there were hundreds of ownerless pigeons of every hue. My companion who was greener than I told me he was fed up with living off the tins of broad beans his mother had given him for the journey. I was equally fed up with my tins of sardines. So, it did not take much to convince me to steal a pigeon from the square. We did so and took it back to the boat, which was, I'm pretty sure, a Turkish one.

We asked the galley assistant to help us cook the bird. The three of us did not have the least idea what sort of meat

150

it was that we held in our hands. We began cooking the odd-looking creature. After five hours of cooking in boiling water, we had to face the fact that there was no way we could stick a fork into the meat of that pigeon: it was harder than stone. The supposed cook was already fed up and easily persuaded us that he had to stop wasting so much fuel, for he was afraid that the great ship would grind to a halt without it. Just as he finished making these stupid remarks, the ship did break down. The 'cook' then got really scared, for it transpired that he believed his own fib. He handed the pot over to us and pushed us out of the galley towards a small storeroom. He wasn't seen for the rest of the voyage. We then learned that this bumpkin was, like us, making his first trip and had only left his native village – somewhere deep in Anatolia – just two days before the ship sailed.

Ah, I confess that we ate the pigeon and as a result spent three days in our berths unable to move with stomach ache, which we blamed on this indigestible meat.

In my memory, I retain only the taste of the meat of that pigeon from Genoa; of those of the Arab world I recall nothing at all. Although I do remember that I liked them.

HAMAM MAHSHI

There's no difference between this and the last recipe (for stuffed chicken), except that you must reduce the cooking time to just 1 hour, plus 15 minutes to brown it. It is eaten with yogurt.

The author and his son with the family of El Akar, the most famous pastry-maker in the Middle East, making kinafa

الفواكه والحلويات

SWEETS, PASTRIES AND DESSERTS

Just as other Mediterranean countries, there's an abundance of every sort of fruit in the Arab world – watermelons, melons, figs, dates, prickly pears etc. On the other hand, desserts and sweets are totally different from those made in northern Mediterranean countries.

You can find a good number of famous cakes, pastries and sweets in all the Arab countries, for example: *katayef, baclawa, kinafa, ruzz bi halib, bastila dulce, maamul, asabeh zeinab, kaab al ghazal*…. There are also all sorts of sweets that belong to distinct regions and countries.

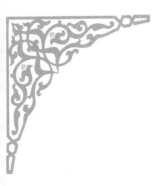

KATAYEF
Sweet little pasties

The enigmatic hermit

Descending that slope	أنزلنا عالسوق نازل
We found an apple	ألقينا تفاحه
An apple so hot and red	حمرا حمرا لفاحه
We swore not to eat it	حلفت ما بآكلها
Till my father and brother's	ليجي خي وبي
Expected return	إجا خي وبَي
They came back together	طلعني عالعليه
Took me to the rooftop	إلقيت شب نايم
I found a young man sleeping	خزيته خزيته
I prodded him awake	وشربت من زيته
At last I drank its juice	زيته تمر حنا
Which tastes of dates and henna	معلق باب الجنه
And is at the gates of Paradise	يا جنه يا ما أحلاك
How precious Paradise is	رب السما خلّك
The God of Heaven created it	فوق السما علاّكَ
And raised it to the Seventh Heaven.	

I hated the few nights of Ramadan when it rained, for then I was deprived of the pleasure of savouring those joyful moments, when the gently warm nights enticed everyone out on to the streets, lit by hundreds of light bulbs winking meaningfully, while my friends and I sang this light-hearted song over and over again, and while thousands and thousands of other Muslim boys and girls in other countries were undoubtedly doing the same.

Holding our lanterns (made from hollowed-out water-melons with holes and a lighted candle mounted inside) we would sing this particular song and some others too.

The *madfaa* of Ramadan or the *ftur* is a harmless cannon shot that signals dusk or sunrise, the moment in which fasting is broken. Its sound reaches every corner of the city. Some children beyond their parents' control (whom I thought were very lucky) would go to watch it. The rest would sit down at the table to eat, but possibly ate nothing, owing to the fact that children don't take part in Ramadan and can eat at any time of day.

'We want *katayef!*' The smallest would start demanding their *katayef*, the classic traditional sweet for every night in the month of Ramadan (without these sweet little pasties, Ramadan would not be the same). Those under the age of twelve did not have to fast, but many did, imitating the adults, or simply to show off. *Katayef* are medieval delicacies and are spread throughout the Muslim empire, including southern Italy and Al-Andalus (Muslim Spain), where even there they are made. The adults didn't make an issue of the children, since they themselves were immersed in a huge quantity of appetising dishes, which were prepared every day throughout the whole month. (The extravagance in which Muslims customarily indulge themselves during this month is a scandal, and surely quite the opposite of the complete mutual austerity that the Prophet Muhammad recommended.) In fact the children clamour impatiently for their *katayef*, first of all because they like them and secondly because when they've finished them it signals the end of the meal, and the beginning of nighttime fun and games on the streets. This is why the children are in such a hurry to eat those little pasties.

Once out in the streets, the children never stop playing. They sing, run, and stand under neighbours' windows begging, pleading for sweets; sometimes they are given them, and at other times all they get is a big bucket of water over their heads. Nothing offends them. It's all part of the much longed-for ingredients that go to make up the joyful evenings of Ramadan. Tiny children of four and five years old wander till the early hours of the morning through the narrow alleyways of the old part of the city. One of the favourite places I liked going to on these nocturnal wanderings of Ramadan was the *zauyet el sheij Nazmi*, a meeting place for dervishes and sufis, led by the famous, enigmatic Sheik Nazmi. He was surrounded by a wealth of unlikely popular legend. At times the locals believed he was a *wili* (a sort of saint), and at others he was accused of womanising, tomfoolery and also of being a *gasus* (spy) for the Jews. Popular imagination has no bounds.

In the Near East there are the very famous frivolous, satirical implorations and short prayers, attributed to Sheik Nazmi and his followers:

Sheikh Nasmi!	شيـخ نـظمـي
The beautiful woman	شـوف الحلوة
Looks in the window	عـالطـاقة
She sees us and she eyes us	عم تطلع حلاقـه
Brothers	يـا اخوان
Hide, I see her, I see her	اغرشـوا شـايـفها
I'm looking at the moon.	القمـورة شـايـفها

I never heard the dervishes chant this type of thing, although I could hardly have been completely certain. For my attention was focused elsewhere, mainly on the delicious *katayef* they offered their visitors, and on their ceaseless whirling to the sound of devilish drums. Nevertheless conservative Muslims and out and out detractors of Sufism insisted on discrediting him.

Frequently we would return home at three in the morning, only two hours before *madfaa el suhur*, the cannon fire set off to awaken believers (and annoyingly, non-believers) to eat something so that they could withstand the following day. If the cannon fire didn't succeed in waking them, the *Musaharatti* would. This altruistic person, who was a tradition of the month of Ramadan, would dedicate himself every morning to running through the streets of the city or village with a big drum (generally a big drum was used, but sometimes other instruments), getting on everyone's nerves with the following message:

Those of you who're sleeping   يا نايمين
Say: He is Allah, the Only One   وحدوا الله
Boom, boom, boom...

This drummer's message has a very deliberate motive. The fundamental basis of Muslim religion is the uniqueness of Allah and this must be remembered at every moment. If someone were asleep, he would not be able to do so, and so he had to be woken up.

Because of the cannon fire and the *Musaharatti*, the vast majority of adults did not move out of their beds until it was time to go to work. In contrast, the children did get up. I remember my brothers and myself almost sleepwalking to the icebox and gobbling down these sweet little pasties, and then going back to bed again. Two hours later everyone was at school.

Everything I've mentioned happens in similar fashion all over the Arab world. The *Ramadaniyat* (nights of Ramadan) are just as splendid in the streets of Cairo, Fez, Meknés, Damascus...

Katayef is eaten less in the Maghreb, but instead *mshabake* (tangles) and *kaab el ghazal* (gazelle horns) are very traditional in the region. Both are sickeningly sweet.

Ramadan is a lunar month and lasts 29 or 30 days. It is eagerly awaited, long-lasting and unforgettable for all Muslims, whether or not they are believers.

Katayef is made up of three components which are prepared separately but eaten together. The outer case, the filling, and the syrup.

KATAYEF
Sweet pasties

Ingredients

Outer cases

(This is the most complicated part, so many families opt to buy them ready made)

1 cup plain flour
½ cup fine semolina
1½ cups water
½ dessertspoon fast baker's yeast, diluted in ¼ cup warm water
1 pinch salt
1 pinch bicarbonate of soda
samneh *for cooking*

Filling

100 grams (4 oz) chopped walnuts, chopped smaller but not ground
1 teaspoon ground cinnamon
2 dessertspoons sugar
1 pinch of ground nutmeg

Syrup

There is no syrup that pleases everyone because the taste is based on the degree of intensity of sweetness, savouriness or tartness that is to everyone's personal taste. I personally follow this formula.

1 cup sugar
½ cup water
¼ cup of orange blossom or rose water
5 drops lemon juice

Method

- Beat all the ingredients for the outer cases in a beater, until it becomes a homogenous and slightly spongy cream. Leave to rest for 20-30 minutes maximum.
- Cook the outer casing on a tray or in a pre-heated non-stick frying pan in the form of pancakes. Gradually pour the dough for the base into the centre of the frying pan and when it has spread to a diameter of 8-10 cm (3-4 inches) and a thickness of 1-2 mm (very thinly), cook for 3-5 minutes or until the bottom of the pancake is just golden (only one side is cooked).
- Meanwhile, prepare the hashueh (filling). There are various types of filling, white cheese, grated coconut, cottage cheese (North Africa and Syria). These last need no special preparation. On the other hand, the most commonly eaten filling – made with walnuts – requires careful preparation.

- For the walnut filling, mix all the ingredients together on a plate and set aside.

- To prepare the syrup, heat the water in a saucepan over moderate heat, and then add the sugar, stir until this has fully melted and continue till it reaches boiling point. Withdraw the saucepan from the heat for 1 minute and then add the drops of lemon juice. Return the saucepan to the heat and boil a second time. When it is boiling, add the orange blossom water or rose water and stir the contents again until it boils for the third time. Then remove from the heat for good. It is served hot.
- Collect the pancakes, golden side down, and place on each 2 teaspoonful of filling, fold it in half and press the edges so that they stick together and the golden side is visible, the whole forming a half-moon shape.

- *Brush the pasties with* samneh *and range them in rows with 1 cm (½ inch) between them, on an oven tray. Put the tray in the oven at 180°C (350°F, Gas 4) for 15 minutes or until they are golden brown. Take out of the oven and serve on individual plates. Finally, sprinkle them (to taste) with the hot syrup and enjoy. Listen, the Arabs don't sprinkle them in syrup, they drown them in it.*

It's advisable to use baking sheets because of their greater capacity for cooking a large number of pasties. Remember that when a family gets together in the Arab world, there are usually a lot of people, so that in a party of just two or three families in a Ramadan social gathering, the number of people shoots up and if each eats 4-5 pasties, you can imagine how many batches of *katayef* are needed. So, with so many mouths to feed, the answer is either to use enormous baking sheets, or to buy the pancakes ready-made.

It is touching to confirm that, despite the difficulties that exist for many, the end of Ramadan makes people sad. But fortunately the day after finishing the month of fasting the most important festivals are celebrated in the Muslim calendar, the *eid el fitr.* During these three feast days, the best dishes are eaten (lambs, chickens, pigeons, etc., stuffed and roasted) and the traditional pastries for that feast – *maamul* and the famous *baklawas* in many different varieties, sweet *bastila* etc.

MAAMUL

This is made from a dough, composed of a mixture of flour, semolina and butter, and divided into portions which are filled with walnuts, pistachios and dates. These are then baked in the oven and finally sprinkled with icing sugar.

BAKLAWAS

The fillings for these are made with a base of syrup or honey, with walnuts, pistachios or almonds. The filling is spread between two layers of filo pastry. It is cut into portions and then baked in the oven.

BASTILA DULCE

This is a delicious north African pastry of Andalusian origin. It is made with puff pastry with a filling made from milk and almonds and sprinkled with icing sugar and cinnamon.

I recommend you buy these ready made from a pâtisserie.

The first day of the *eid* begins with *salat el eid* (dawn prayer and short prayers). It is the most moving and symbolic moment of the celebrations. What must be done next is to visit the cemeteries and it is there that one begins to eat the first pastries. After paying their respects to the dead, people immediately leave. From then on, everyone is converted into host and guest, and some real races begin to visit the maximum number of relations and friends. Each one of these visits cannot last any more than twenty to thirty minutes (if you have more time you can visit more people). On each visit you have to accept the pastries the host offers you. When midday arrives, the big meal is eaten, which is traditionally the best of the year. After lunch, visits continue and naturally so do the pastries and the coffees.

In all, there are three consecutive days of continuous gorging, meal upon meal, pastries, coffee and tea.

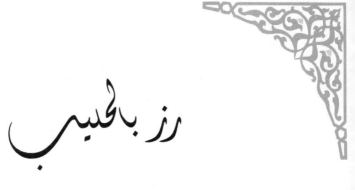

RUZZ BIL-HALIB
Rice with milk

'You can have all the rice you want and more, but you'll not get milk on its own! If you want some rice with a bit of milk, that's fine. I'll make you some right away.' This was often what mothers said to their children when they asked for some milk to drink. In towns, in those difficult years of the 1950s and 1960s, milk was something more than a luxury; in fact it was a real medicine and only sick people from the upper classes drank it. So, you may ask ingenuously, what did children have for breakfast? Every day, until the age of five, they basically drank their mother's milk. From that age onwards, and also before, they began to eat the same as the adults. And every day, at breakfast and dinnertime they had – and still do – two or three cups of tea.

There were times, particularly during the popular revolts of the 1960s, when Arab governments and UNRWA[13] distributed powdered milk to schoolchildren – to keep the public happy. Thirty-five years later I can still recall that milk's repugnant smell. Nevertheless under the teacher's threat we drank that substance that afterwards made everyone ill.

I remember vaguely only one occasion when my family bought milk to drink. It was when the barber was carrying out a *Thur* (circumcision) on my small brother. He cried dreadfully he was in so much pain, but he was immensely happy, mostly because of all the presents he received on this eventful occasion and, ah! he had fresh goat's milk because my mother (just like all mothers) could not suckle a child confined to bed.

Faced with such lavish treatment no child would want to get better. And so the period of his convalescence lasted, exaggeratedly, for more than a month, during which the circumcised child never stopped receiving presents, the best food, the best drink, the best clothing, and the worst feelings of envy from his siblings.

Very often bakeries cook their neighbours' pastries for them

Once our parents decided to bring that excessive pampering to a close, they began to persuade the child that he was now a man and that all the pampering was for baby children. Why parents behaved like this was not, as a general rule, because the child was being a nuisance, but because of the excessive taunting that came from the other children (which basically was simply from jealousy). They would torment him and call him a spoilt brat who was as weak as a girl, or who needed as much milk as a newborn baby. The child finally reacted and outwardly gave up liking all the things that only a few hours before he'd really enjoyed. He then started to imitate grown-up men, put on long trousers, run errands, protect his sisters and to eat and drink like the men. The men drank tea, never milk; and so, the child did likewise.

So am I saying Arabs never use milk products? Clearly they do, and very much so, but preserved products (in the form of cheeses) or cooked (in puddings, like rice with milk). This last dish is as old as rice itself; it was well known by Hindus, Persians, Arabs, and Greeks and is made in thousands of ways. The Arab recipe (the modern one) which demands a great deal of patience, is as follows.

RUZZ BI HALIB
Rice with milk

Serves 8-10

Ingredients

8 cups milk
1 cup rice, medium size
1 cup sugar
½ teaspoon mestaka *(indispensable granules with an aromatic*

thickening capacity. They are sold in Middle Eastern shops)
⅓ cup of orange blossom water
ground cinnamon
honey
½ cup pistachios (unsalted and chopped – optional)
desiccated coconut (optional)
pieces of caramelised walnut (optional)
The optional ingredients give the dish a lot of prestige.

Method

- *Clean the rice well and leave it to soak in hot water for 1 hour. Then rinse it and put it in a saucepan with a cup of water over moderate heat.*
- *10 minutes later, add the milk and turn the heat down. Stir constantly with a wooden spoon for ¾ hour.*
- *Add the sugar and continue stirring.*
- *Mix the* mestaka *granules with a spoonful of sugar and mash them up into powder. Then add them to the saucepan and continue stirring for a further 5 minutes.*
- *Add the orange blossom water and continue stirring for 2 more minutes.*
- *Remove the saucepan from the heat and immediately turn out the contents into small dishes or small tubs.*
- *Leave to cool and then put them in the refrigerator for 3 hours before eating them.*
- *At the time of serving, and of course when they are cold, decorate the surface with fine trickles of honey and sprinkle with pistachios, coconut, cinnamon and finally top with pieces of caramelised walnut.*

VARIATIONS

There are a number of variations of this recipe, as well known as the original all over the Arab world.

MHALABIEH

This takes half the time of the previous recipes and you substitute the rice with cornstarch diluted in ½ small cup of hot water.

MHALABIEH MAA BURTUQAL
with oranges

Before pouring the cooked *mhalabieh* into the little dishes, you add a layer of orange juice cooked with a little cornstarch.

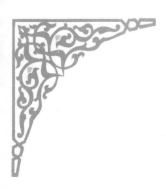

I HAVE WEPT

I have wept…yet I weep not for footprints
Vanished in the desert, in the empty quarter.
And yet I am afflicted by a great dead love,
Nor do I weep for cruel exile far from my belovèd.
But the traditions they set forth –
Those pious Companions of our great Prophet –
Have caused my tears to stream
Like a mighty torrent down my throat.
For they forbade us to drink wine.
From then till now this prohibition lives.
And since wine has been condemned
It is for wine's fate that I weep.
And I drink it undiluted, knowing very soon
I shall be punished for my sin.
I feel those eighty lashes raining on my back.

Abu-Nowas, ninth century

DRINKS

AL MASHRUBAT
Cold drinks

Veneration of water

WATER

For Muslims there is nothing more delicious, healthy, beautiful and sacred than water. It is the only drink that will rid you of thirst. In the message of the Koran, Allah said: 'With water have I created all living things.' In the Koran and in the *Hadith* (the traditions and sayings of the Prophet Muhammad), there are numerous incitements to believers to venerate water, not to foul it, nor squander it, nor deprive anyone of it.

As the tourist wanders through the streets of Arab towns and villages, he or she is often left amazed by the enormous number of houses and shops that have in their entrances earthenware pitchers or large jars of water to offer to passersby in the name of Allah and his Prophet.

It was about thirty years ago when I came to live in Europe. After so many years, I believe I've come to assimilate every European custom, except one, and I shall probably never accept that. This is the custom of paying money for water in bars, in countries which are awash with water.

It may well be that the scarcity of water in a great part of the Arab world has given rise to an exaggerated devotion and high doses of superstition with regard to its springs. For example, the great majority bear the name of a prophet or saint. Also, people never go to the spring to collect water after sunset, since it's believed that springs are looked after by certain angels or saints, and at that time of the day they're tired, so people only fetch their water during the day. If they did the opposite and irritated the guardians of the springs, they would dry up immediately. In Nazareth (Palestine), as a thank you for the spring of water near their city and named after the Virgin Mary, Christian Arabs make offerings of flowers, lighted candles and prayers.

One of the most bizarre tales about water is that told by the inhabitants of the villages around Lake Tiberiades (on the frontier of Jordan and Palestine). It concerns the hot water bubbling up from the hot springs that abound in that region. The locals, including my own family, insist that the prophet-king Suleiman (Solomon) ordered the spirits and demons to heat the water. They obeyed the order and while they were doing it they became blind and deaf. So when the time came they did not hear of the death of their friend and overlord. Consequently, they've continued to heat the water ever since.

Bismi Allah ar-Rahman ar-Rahim (in the name of Allah, the Merciful and Compassionate). This is the phrase Muslim-Arabs always recite before drinking or taking water. The Christian Arabs, under their influence, also recite the same phrase, though less frequently, when they bless themselves. Then they drink water in small quantities, a little at a time and never gulp it, for they know that speed is one of *Shaittan*'s (Satan's) habits.

There is always water on the meal table. It is generally served by the youngest of those present. The host would not feel humbled if he did it himself, quite the reverse (proving the Arab proverb that says that the servant of the tribe shall be its chief), meaning that humility will raise his status.

When an Arab asks for a glass of water to drink, he always does so by eulogising the person serving him and offering him the following wish: 'Give me water that Allah in turn may give you water from Zamzam.' Zamzam is Islam's most sacred well, situated near Mecca and Medina. All the pilgrims drink this water.

I should like to advise anyone travelling to the Arab countries that in many regions there is a custom of adding a little orange blossom or rose water to the water. Why? My uncle, Sheikh Ahmed, chief of Islamic Shariha (laws) in Cairo, Amman and Nablus, tells me that it is because the Prophet Muhammad blessed the light meal that finished with a glass of water, because it is a good aid to digestion, a diuretic, and eliminates bad breath. Naturally, it follows that if the water is scented it is even better. This habit has still not been abandoned, notwithstanding the common use of toothpaste nowadays.

AIRAN

Airan is the classic drink of the Bedouin of Asia Minor. It is offered as a refreshment, especially in summer. It stimulates the appetite, so that barely has the guest arrived than he is offered a glass of *airan*.

The first *airan* I ever had was as the result of an accident caused through Arab mythology. We had stopped at the 'house' of a semi-stationary Bedouin on the Saudi-Iraqi border, and he insisted on offering us some refreshment when he learned that the passengers my cousin was carrying in his minibus were Iraqi pilgrims returning home from Mecca. The Bedouin claimed that he would achieve *thawab* (the blessing of Allah) through his help to the pilgrims.

His 'house' was built entirely of adobe and consisted of one single room, in which he offered the most comfortable seats to the oldest present and in second place to those who were related to these elderly people. So, a child of thirteen like myself, an assistant to the driver, naturally had the worst seat, near but not close to the demon-infested, accursed doorway of his only living room. The base of the threshold of a house was, according to popular belief, inhabited by the *Djinn* and *Shayatin* (evil spirits and Satans); what is more it was never advisable to be near a threshold, not even to pause as you entered or left the house, for fear of provoking the Satans.

Immediately after we had all sat down, the Bedouin sent his small son of ten to look for the drinks that his wife, who had scarcely seen us, was preparing in her *jaima* (tent). Several moments passed and the child returned with a large tray in his hands. But when the poor child came to jumping over the threshold to enter the living room, he let go of the tray of glasses full to the brim with the white drink and it fell right on top of me. I was feeling very thirsty and licked all the liquid off that was on my face, without giving a thought to the uproar mounting in the living room. And that was the first time I tasted *airan*.

AIRAN
Bedouin drink

Serves 4

Ingredients

3 yogurts
3 cups water
2 small sprigs fresh mint
1 peeled garlic
1 teaspoon salt
2-3 ice cubes (This last ingredient is a recent addition to the drink and is only found in towns)

Method

- *Put all the ingredients in a large jug and stir with a long spoon, until you have a kind of syrupy consistency.*

In the Arab repertoire of drinks, you can find all kinds of drinks that can be made at home, using as a base, liquorice, carob beans, oranges and tamarind (Indian dates), grapes, sultanas. Nowadays these drinks are offered as refreshments and almost never served with food.

ARAQ

This alcoholic drink, similar to those with an aniseed base, warrants a special mention. Despite its prohibition throughout the Arab world, it has never totally disappeared from either legal or illegal markets. It is a drink that is inseparable from the famous *mezza*,[15] which is well known in Asia Minor, especially in Lebanon and Turkey. There is in these countries a resident Armenian minority, whose members are true masters at creating this drink, using rice and a small amount of aniseed as basic ingredients. When drunk, it is normally diluted in a little water, or perhaps not. It should be taken in small quantities, as if it were vodka or sherry.

Araq along with *mezza* or *mejana*[16] form the 'triad' with which Arabs identify the Lebanese. In the popular imagination, every Arab country has its 'triad' to identify itself. For example, Egypt has the singer Um Kulthum, *mdammas* (beans) and the final element is that the Egyptians are always unsophisticated. Algeria has a lot of natural gas, a million martyrs (from their war of Independence) and, thirdly, the people don't speak Arabic. Yemen has *qat* (hallucinogenic grass), daggers and, finally, goats. Jordan has....

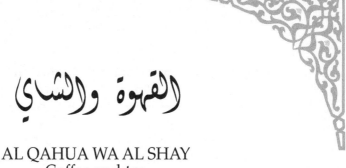

القهوة والشاي

AL QAHUA WA AL SHAY
Coffee and tea

Tragi-comic true stories

In our small dwelling, we were all jam-packed around our little *mankal* (brazier). There were fourteen of us in our family: ten brothers and sisters, my parents, my aunt and my maternal grandmother. My father, who represented 'authority', always occupied the best seat closest to the fire and directed everything that had to be done regarding that multipurpose, miraculous contraption. The brazier was no more than 50 cm (19½ inches) long and 30 cm (12 inches) across, and every winter our lives revolved around it; it was the only warm place in the house, we cooked on it, chatted round it, my mother dried her washing there and among all this 'overbooking', my brothers tried to study as best they could. The 1950s were hard years, when my parents down-sized from being prosperous merchants in Palestine to simple refugees.

My mother would place the big spouted pot on a corner of the brazier, while my father who was closest to it, schooled by bitter experience not to make a false move, dextrously manoeuvred a large pair of tongs. He would insert four of five squares of goat's cheese – which we'd preserved ourselves – on to its prongs and then place the tongs on the live coals of the *mancal*, so that we had toasted goat's cheese. Without touching the tongs, he would mount the *mansab* (a support shaped like a rather high crown) over them, and on this he would toast the bread. At breakfast or dinner, he would dole out a share to each of us of a piece of bread, a piece of cheese and a cup of tea. Often there was no cheese, and then it was substituted with the famous *zeit y zaatar* (a mixture of oregano, salt, sesame and *summak*). The bread would be smeared with oil, and then sprinkled on top with the *zaatar*. After that, the bread would be toasted on the brazier to make the well-known *manúshe*. During winter we toasted the little pieces of bread, but in summer we didn't make this. But even then, the tea was always served piping hot.

Tea was popularised in the Near East by the English. In the nineteenth century it was totally unknown by the great majority of Arabs in the region. On the other hand, the Maghrebi and Saharians have drunk tea for many decades before.

So it's no surprise that in the North African Maghreb, tea is surrounded in ritual and anecdote. Nevertheless its inclusion into the list of beverages drunk in the Middle East is recent and here such rituals and anecdotes are in short supply. The same cannot be said of coffee, which is a drink/infusion of irrefutable Arab origin, or at least of Middle Eastern origin. Much has been written about its discovery and the shepherd called el Khaldi, who observed his goats' excitement on eating that plant and its fruits, that later would be known as *kalwa* or *qahwa* (coffee). Naturally, because of its antiquity, the history of coffee has a great number of anecdotes, rituals and stories, some of them fraught with tragi-comic situations.

Sitting around the brazier, we heard various stories about coffee and two of them were truly difficult to believe, but they are nonetheless true. The first had quite a comic ending. It all came about through adventurers from foreign lands not knowing about local customs. In the second decade of the twentieth century, an Englishman on an expedition arrived in the desert that lies between Jordan and Saudi Arabia, and was received by a Bedouin chief in his tent. The Englishman was ill informed on the rites of hospitality among Arabs, and especially among the Bedouin. He knew, for example, of the offence that would be caused by refusing a coffee offered by an Arab, but on the other hand did not have the remotest idea that, if he did not wish to have any more coffee he had to turn his cup upside down before leaving it in the tray. The Englishman was apprised of this detail only after having drunk twenty-six cups of coffee. The poor adventurer could not sleep for a week afterwards. In fact he did not know – my grandmother told me – if his insomnia was caused by the excitement that the coffee produced in him, or by the gripes and diarrhoea produced by its excessive consumption in so short a space of time.

The second story had a more tragic finale, owing to the numerous conflicting interpretations made by Bedouin of their countless rituals and traditions. It happened in the nineteenth century. A young Bedouin, returning home, found his wife seated with a stranger in the *jaima* (Bedouin tent) erected in the middle of the desert; the young man immediately leapt out of the tent and ran straight to his mother's where he questioned her on the number of cups of coffee the guest had had. 'Three,' his mother said. The young man returned to his tent where his wife and the guest were, and, without a word, slit both their throats. The author of this double crime justified his actions before a tribal tribunal, by excusing himself with an epic verse (not so long ago in the past, these verses and refrains were an authentic edict, expressing as they did rules of law that were imposed ruthlessly in the desert). This verse went as follows:

> *The offering of the first coffee is a duty to the guest.*
> *The second coffee is for the purpose of enjoyment.*
> *And, if it reaches a point where a third coffee is served, the sword*
> *is the remedy.*

The young man wrongly interpreted this Bedouin verse and at the tribunal said that the situation had to end that way because he had had to defend his honour, since his wife, being on her own, should have offered only one coffee once, and then the guest should have left, bearing in mind that the *rab el beit* (the god of the house – the husband) was absent. By offering the man a second coffee, for the purpose of enjoyment, as the saying went, unhesitatingly, he deduced that there had been a good chemistry between them; in other words the *wilie* (the unresisting woman) and the foreigner were seeking pleasure, for what he had done he did in order to clear his own honour and that of his tribe.

The most likely interpretation of this piece of verbiage is that the first coffee that the host offers is to honour the guest (or guests); the second is a signal that those present begin to enjoy the get-together and the party (the enjoyment), and if it comes to taking a third coffee, it is because they have arrived at a level of friendship that will be defended on both sides by the sword. Another version exists that also treats of the polemical third line. It says that if a woman, whose husband is absent, gets to the point of offering the third coffee to a foreigner or guest, that person should be ready to protect the woman with his sword till her husband returns.

Innumerable are the stories, traditions, superstitions that surround coffee in the Arab world; to relate all of them would fill several books But, before finishing and summing up, I would like to mention various details relating to coffee, that will doubtless be useful for travellers in those regions.

In general, taking a cup of coffee signifies the beginning or the end of an agreeable stay, visit, blow-out, wedding, business deal, etc.

On everyday visits, the host serves the first coffee of welcome immediately, and repeats *ad infinitum* *'Ahla u sahla'* (greetings of welcome) to make it quite clear that this coffee is not the coffee that signifies departure. The second coffee signifies the end of the visit. However, a good Arab never serves the second coffee if the visitor does not request it; the visitor addressing his hosts will say: 'If you will permit, coffee, it's time to leave.' Everything depends on the level of affinity and appreciation the host feels towards the guest. If he feels a great deal, he delays serving the coffee to the departing guest, but if he feels little, it will be done in a few seconds.

Arab women will often stand in for their menfolk in their absence, and so between other duties the Arab wife must fulfil this rule of hospitality. In such a situation, it is pleasing and very chivalrous if the visitor amiably refuses the coffee offered by the woman and leaves. In Palestinian villages, the women are very insistent on offering coffee; so then, faced with their stubbornness, you must take it, but with extreme brevity and always in the entrance to the house, never inside.

Taking coffee with an enemy or refusing it is a sign of peace or the continuation of a dispute respectively. In times not so far distant, agreements were not signed on paper but only by taking coffee.

When a *jaha* (emissary or messenger) goes to the family of a girl to ask for her hand in marriage, he takes great care not to take coffee before his petition is satisfied. Leaving an Arab's house without taking coffee is considered insulting to the host. For this reason, the Bedouin – known for his innate wisdom – often intuits the motive of the visits and succeeds in avoiding that insult by offering coffee immediately to see if the emissaries rise to the bait and take it. If they do, he will insure him own reputation, with a margin of manoeuvre to refuse or accept the emissaries' petition, without the risk of losing face because the *jaha* did not consume the first and principal requisite of hospitality in his house. This often happens with ingenuous townspeople when, unthinkingly, they immediately accept the coffee offered by the suspicious Bedouin. They do not realise that, by agreeing so precipitately, they will in all probability return home empty-handed and without being able to speak ill of him. This detail never passes unnoticed among the Bedouin themselves.

If they intend to ask for something when they come, they refuse the coffee in a friendly way: '*Inshaalah baadein* [with the will of Allah, we shall take it later]', they say. In other words, whether we have coffee or not, the outcome is still to be settled.

Real Arab coffee should be bitter, with no sugar, although in fact bitter coffee is only served after finishing a good blow-out or in ceremonies of mourning. The inclusion of sugar in coffee is recent and disturbs the authentic aroma of the coffee. Although it seems incredible, if an old person passes away, the relations of the dead person offer people who turn up with messages of condolence coffee with sugar. The interpretations of this detail are, as always, disparate. The first and most probable says that the relations must sweeten the mouth of all those present, as a sign of satisfaction, because the old person made good use of a good long innings. The second, according to spiteful tongues, refers to the happiness of the relations for the fact that they have unburdened themselves of an old person.

You may ask why Arabs feel such affection and passion for coffee? It may be because of an old legend that says that the drink was made by the Angel Gabriel and offered, for the first time in the history of mankind, to the Prophet Muhammad. Nevertheless, the only written evidence about the discovery of coffee refers to the shepherd el Khaldi, and the first to drink the classic infusion we know today was the dervish Shazly el adrusy in the tenth century.

Yemen was the country in which coffee originated, although several authors have attributed its origin to Ethiopia. *Al mukhá* (Mocca) coffee, in the region of the Red Sea and around Aden (Yemen) is truly unbeatable. The Yemeni merchant caravans were responsible for spreading coffee into the rest of the Arabian peninsula, Syria, Turkey and from there to Europe. Since then, its cultivation has spread through a number of countries with climates similar to the Yemen. And speaking of the Yemen, if dear readers you get the chance to visit this most genuine of Arab countries (the rest are Arabised), do make an effort to try to take part in some *Sanaaí* celebration of song. These begin immediately after lunch and continue until nightfall, which is known as the hour of the prophet Suleiman, a time when people should devote themselves to reflection. There are three phases to the celebration: the reception, singing and dreaming awake, and finally, reflection, and during all three, the participants never stop singing and making music for one moment, chewing *qat* (a hallucingenic drug) and, why not!, drinking the best coffee in the world.

In some regions, the reverence, passion and longing for coffee reach unbelievable levels of true delirium. The anthropologist Hanauer found in tombs of tribal chieftains in the Negev and Sinai deserts, that beside the bodies of their owners lay *bakraj* (coffee pots), *mihmasa* (coffee roasters) and various typical utensils used in preparing coffee.

In the same way, coffee fanatics often swear on the life of Shazly, the first person to make the drink.

Arab coffee is almost always served with some cardamom added. If a wife adds too much of this aphrodisiac, it provokes much suggestive and promiscuous comment...we have touched on this theme in the chapter on *Tabbouleh*.

The host should taste the coffee before offering it, and when offering it always begin on the right, except if someone proposes that the oldest male should be served first. Sometimes he will agree, sometimes not, making a grand gesture of modesty and a reference to the traditional code that says: 'Serve from the right, even though Abu Zeid [a heroic nobleman of Arab mythology] is present.'

While the Middle East has an endless supply of anecdotes about coffee, there are few in North Africa. Here, on the other hand, is an abundance of stories about tea. This is because there was little Arab or later Ottoman influence in that region, as it was colonised at an early date by Europeans (who were more attuned to tea, because it was readily available from their other south Asian colonies).

I've been to various regions in Arab North Africa and made contact with the people there, both indigenous and emigrants – who would slip easily into reverie and pass on their fascinating colourful stories, of which the best known and splendid is gently told by the *Sahrauíin* as they offer their guest three glasses of tea. The first has a very bitter taste, which, they say is like life itself; the second has a neutral flavour – like love, as you cannot tell whether it is bitter or sweet, and the last is very sweet – like death. This last comment often provokes laughter among the *Tuareg* (the blue men from the south of Algeria), who insist that no one has ever returned from death to confirm that it is as sweet as all that.

They usually drink *shay ajdar* (green tea) in the Maghreb, though this type of tea is little known in the *Mashrek* (the eastern Arab world). There, classic black tea is the one that is most consumed.

Both types are prepared in completely different ways. In the Maghreb, the process is more ritualistic and slow, while in the East, owing to tea's inferior status vis à vis coffee, little attention is given to its preparation.

In fact there is nothing so fascinating as spending a social evening in a Bedouin tent, reclining on colourful striped rugs, with ones elbow resting on silken cushions, contemplating a totally clear sky, spangled with stars and incredibly close. I had the good fortune to spend some immensely alarming nights in the Dahna desert which borders on the western shores of the Arabian Gulf and is connected to the vast Rub el jali desert – the Empty Quarter – thousands and thousands of square miles of nothing.

Beside a *bakraj al qahwa* (a tall copper pot for preparing

coffee, with a narrow neck and broad base), a Bedouin woman was busily intent on discerning our future by reading the pictures left by the coffee grains in our cups after she had turned them upside down. Every night we were accompanied by a *badaui* (Bedouin) who sang and played the poignant *rabab*[17] marvellously and who had never studied music. The Bedouin's voice, no less heartrending than his instrument, rang out from our tent, cleaving infinity in that immense desert. Over and over he sang:

She sneered at my grey hair	عيرتني بـالشيب
And showed no respect	وهو وقار
If only she'd reproached me	ليتها عيرتني
For a real sin!	بما هو عار
Have you forgotten the stars	إنتكن شابت الزوائد منـي
Light up the darkened sky?[18]	فالليالي تزينها الأقمار

It's no exaggeration to say that in Arab countries there are dozens of types of coffee and dozens of ways of preparing them. And it's certainly true to say that in the region where coffee originated, methods of cultivation, harvesting, transportation, roasting and packing are all of primary importance in determining the quality of the coffee as a raw material. Arabs, however, believe absolutely that in order to make an excellent cup of coffee, the *nak* (soul) that each person adds as they prepare it, is much more important than all the factors that have gone before. So what do Arabs mean when they talk of the soul? Here, they simply mean the care with which the coffee is prepared, and the longing to drink it. Requisites such as these illustrate the character and disposition of the host towards his guest. One of those strange things which greatly surprised me in the Western world was and still is the automatic speed with which Europeans and North Americans make and drink their coffee in the blink of an eye. I've repeatedly asked myself how they can go into a bar, and often by themselves, remain standing and not utter a word, and in one minute gulp down a coffee that's almost lacking any aroma, is bitter and heartless, and on top of that isn't even served in a proper cup.

I remember as a child seeing my mother at one of her *istikbals*[19] discussing the types of coffee and the cleverness such and such a woman had in making it. The majority of the women – whose opinion in this matter is undisputed – said that the *adani* coffee from Aden (Yemen) was unsurpassed (they did not then know of the worldwide term, 'Mocca', nor of the two types of coffee: Arabica and Robusta). And they added that no one could better the Bedouin in roasting it with the *mihmasa* (primitive roaster) or grinding it with the *mihbash* (a wooden mortar), or preparing it, not even the Turks.

The Turks themselves say that there are three basic conditions for a really enjoyable, good coffee: it must as black as hell (they are referring to the black fate of the sinner and not to hell itself, for in Muslim mythology, hell – *Jahannan Al Hamra* – is a gigantic brazier with live flames and so has the colour red), as strong as death, and as sweet as love.

The four most frequent tastes made in the Arab world are as follows:

Sada: with no sugar

Jafif: with a little sugar

Osmaly (Ottoman or Turkish): medium sweet

and finally, *Al Riha*: to which only 'the aroma' of the sugar is added, in other words, less than the minimum.

To all these cardamom is always added, a special, primordial spice for making Arab coffee. If cardamom is omitted, you will have some sort of coffee, but not Arab coffee.

AL QAHWA
Coffee

Serves 4

Ingredients

4 cups of natural water, free of any flavour
0-4 medium sized spoonfuls of sugar (according to taste)
6 medium-sized spoonfuls of ground Arab coffee (mixed with cardamom). If you can't obtain this coffee, you can prepare it fairly simply by roasting 4 green cardomom pods, adding 8 spoonfuls of coffee beans (already roasted) and grinding them as finely as you can. This will be enough for 4 cups.

Method

- *In a suitable pot or saucepan, heat the water to make the coffee. When it is medium hot, add the desired quantity of sugar and once the sugar is dissolved add the coffee and stir with a spoon continuously. At the end of several minutes, you will notice the contents of the saucepan rising to the top.*
- *At that moment withdraw the pot from the heat, before it boils over. Continue stirring with a spoon for one more minute and put the saucepan back on the heat. Continue stirring with the spoon for 2 more minutes, stop stirring and immediately you will see the contents rising to the top again. At that moment withdraw the coffee from the heat and you will have finished heating it.*
- *The cream that has formed on top of the coffee should be shared equally between the four cups; then pour the rest of the coffee and serve immediately. Nothwithstanding, you should wait two minutes before drinking it to give sufficient time for the grounds to settle at*

the bottom of the cup.

- *If you wish to make it over a proper fire, with live coals, put the pot directly on to the live coals and follow the same steps as previously. But you should multiply the time taken by four. It is certainly worth the trouble.*
- *Never prepare Arab coffee in cafetières of any sort; either you make it as I've described or you don't make it at all.*

NOTE

True Bedouin serve it after it has rested and without cream. Why? And to whom do they serve this? The reason is that the Bedouin always have coffee prepared in readiness for the unexpected visitor or for passersby. Nevertheless coffee will be made the original way at get-togethers for family or for friends.

Lamentably, few authentic Bedouin remain. The motor car has reduced this noble ethnic group to nothing.

PREPARATION OF TEA

Children the world over, no matter where they are, always ask the same curious questions. One of the most common is: who was the first to make such and such a thing?

Like all military men, my uncle General Innab preferred tea to coffee (in the 1940s and 1950s, some Arabs imitated English habits, because it was considered a step towards modernity). One day he was at our house and began getting the brazier ready to put the tea pot cleverly on it. My smallest brother came up with a typical question: who was the first to take the first cup of tea? The ancient tale my uncle told us about the Chinese emperor didn't surprise us in any way. Because the water was impure, the Chinese emperor recommended his subjects to boil it before drinking it. To a Chinese, this story is very well known. While waiting for the water to cool, into the cup fell a leaf of a plant which tinged all the water...This story did not feel very relevant to us. However, we were most attentive and astonished when the general assured us that he was the first to taste tea in the whole of *Sham* (Syria, Lebanon, Jordan and Palestine). It was at the beginning of the twentieth century, when he made his first contact with the English colonialists – he helped a patrol of English soldiers who had problems with their vehicle in the middle of the desert void to the south of Karak in Jordan. As a reward, they gave him a small sack of tea. He was then a young and insignificant commercial traveller and was surprised by the gift and did not know what the plant was. Lacking neither diligence nor bashfulness, he offered some to his mule, which swallowed both the tea and the sack in one go. The English were naturally dumbfounded, explained what it was and offered young Innab a cup of tea.

With his left hand the general deftly removed the lid from the pot – the water was already boiling – while he introduced his right into a square tin decorated with Hindu pictures and which contained loose tea. Murmuring the name of Allah, he took a handful of tea from it, and put it in the pot, returned the lid, and placed the pot immediately on a corner of the brazier, away from the heap of live coals that were always in the centre (with this manoeuvre we deduced that it had to continue brewing, but on a low heat). Five minutes later, General Innab served us the tea in tiny cups, and added to each cup one or two medium-sized spoonfuls of sugar. 'This was how Sergeant Robert made the first tea I ever had and I've always gone on making it the same way,' he said.

In order to make things easier, Arabs often add the sugar to the water while it is boiling. This way, although this may seem like an exaggeration, people are looking to save on the number of individual spoons used, so as not to waste scarce water at washing-up time.

AL SHAY
Tea

For each cup of tea

Ingredients

1 cup of natural water, devoid of any flavour (such a requisite is essential for a good cup of tea)[20]
1 medium-sized spoonful of loose tea. We recommend Ceylon (Sri Lankan) tea, which is functional and generous in character. This recommendation was one oft repeated by my brother-in-law Saadiddin, who was 'king' of tea in a great part of the Middle East, from the 1950s until the 1980s. He praised this tea's good light flavour, its good price, its aroma, its medicinal properties – anti-fever, anti-caries etc. In other words, its generosity of character.
1-2 medium-sized spoons of sugar (to taste)
a fresh leaf of mint or sage (optional) is added to each cup when made.

In the Maghreb everything is different and everyone keeps up the classic ritual for preparing this drink, The Maghrebi continue to give great importance to tea, when they wish to be hospitable or entertain. And so they take great pains preparing it.

MAGHREBI TEA

For 6 cups

Ingredients

1 good sprig of mint or marihuana
1 tablespoon green tea
6 medium-sized spoons sugar
½ litre (just under a pint) natural water

Method

- Put the mint or marihuana in a teapot with the tablespoonful of green tea and sugar.

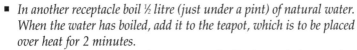

- *In another receptacle boil ½ litre (just under a pint) of natural water. When the water has boiled, add it to the teapot, which is to be placed over heat for 2 minutes.*
- *Lower the heat and leave the pot to rest for 5 minutes before serving the tea in small cups.*

In Algeria, this is the way they made it for me; on the other hand, the Saharians and the Tuareg, with their customary relaxed way of life and lack of modern resources, prepare it with even more ceremony. For a stove they use a contraption similar to an oil lamp with little more than candle power. And at one gathering they will prepare three different sorts of tea. As we mentioned before, the first with no sugar, the second with a moderate amount and the third and last with a lot of sugar.

These are the two main, authentic ways of preparing tea in the Arab world, although many eccentricities exist with other distinctive touches, that are very interesting to taste. For example, adding a small amount of nutmeg or cinnamon to a cup of tea – I've done this – and I've also often added a drop of rose water and 4-5 raw pine kernels to tea.

Today, braziers are in short supply. You can substitute barbecues. If there's no chance of you making tea the artisans' way, you will have to resort to the kitchen stove.

آداب الطعام
في المجتمع العربي الإسلامي

MUSLIM-ARAB RULES FOR COOKING AND BEHAVIOUR AT TABLE

One question that will be floating in everyone's mind is whether or not Muslim-Arabs really follow these rules? Naturally not everyone fulfils them, nor do those who follow them do so rigorously. So where have these rules come from?

First of all, they come from the Koran. Failure to comply with any of these particular rules is considered a sin. Secondly, they come from the *Hadith* (the teachings of the Prophet Muhammad). Compliance with these is held in high regard. And, thirdly, they come from *Taqalid* (customs and traditions). There is moderate compliance with these. Non-compliance is not criticised, but following them earns cultural respect.

The rules are divided into three groups: before eating, during the meal, and after the meal.

Rules before the meal

- Prepare produce for eating and drinking that is legal, that is to say, no pork, produce from which the blood has been removed, no carrion, no hallucinogenic beverage whatsoever, no stolen produce. Except in cases where

193

there is a need to survive, all the above-mentioned remain emphatically forbidden.

- Wash your hands.
- Place the food on a table, which is slightly higher than the ground, out of respect for Allah's happy event. On journeys, the food should be placed on a cloth, blanket, sheet etc.
- Do not use gold or silver utensils.
- Sit decently. Muhammad's favourite positions are sitting on the floor on ones knees, or extending the right leg and sitting on the left. In this position, the stomach is slightly compressed so that you have the sensation of being full, and thus you will curb your eating. Such an attitude reflects the ascetic character of the Prophet, who always recommended moderation at mealtimes to his disciples. Muhammad said: 'Filling a receptacle to the full is a mistake, and if that receptacle is the stomach it will be the worst mistake possible. So then,' the Prophet continued, 'at mealtimes a wise believer should devote a third of the space in his stomach to solid food, a second third to drink and the final third to his soul. Those who follow such a recommendation will never need a doctor.' By the look of it, no one follows this rule.
- One should be in agreement about everything with the person who has the food.
- Good believers never eat on their own. Muhammad says: 'The most blessed table is the one which is covered with many hands.'

Rules during the meal

- *'Bismi Allah ar-Rahman ar-Rahim'* (in the name of Allah, the Compassionate, the Merciful). It is normal practice for all Arabs, whatever their creed (Muslim, Christian and agnostic included) to make this mention of Allah, before beginning anything whatsoever, however insignificant. There are people who repeat this phrase before every mouthful. By so doing they avoid the possibility that the enjoyment of the meal might make them forget God.

- You must not begin your meal before the oldest person present begins his.
- Eat with your right hand.
- 'Begin eating with a little salt or dates.' So said Ali (a co-religionary of Muhammad and the fourth caliph). 'Whoever follows this advice will be taking precautions against 70 different illnesses and will eliminate all the bugs inside his stomach.' In the North African Maghreb and in the Arabian peninsula it is a common practice to begin the meal with a date; on the other hand, you will not see this done in the Middle East.
- Mouthfuls should be small and well masticated to facilitate digestion. You cannot begin the next mouthful before you have swallowed the first, for impatience is one of Satan's habits. For the same reason, it is looked down on to blow on hot food to cool it. You must arm yourself with patience and wait.
- If the dishes are communal (that is, there are no individual plates), you should eat from the side of the dish nearest you.
- You do not have to watch or pay special attention to other people's manners, because you must not embarrass them.
- If some food falls to the floor, you must pick it up, clean it and eat it. If it is difficult to clean, you must give it to an animal rather than throw it away; otherwise Satan will take it. Pay special attention to bread. Never have I seen an Arab, be he Muslim or Christian, throw away or even push away a crust of bread. This includes when a piece of bread falls on the floor: he will immediately pick it up so that nobody treads on it, kiss it and raise it to his forehead

as a sign of respect. If it happens in reasonable conditions, he will eat it or give it to an animal; in other circumstances, he will hide it in a hole far from Satan's reach.

- Masticate and swallow in silence and do not make tiresome noises. You should make conversation during the meal, but always on agreeable subjects.
- Never belch. Should you do so, you should beg pardon, *asef, afwan*. The English word 'sorry' is also acceptable.

Rules for the end of the meal

- The first point I would like to make here has a bearing on the one just mentioned above. This is a topic that has been distorted by ill-informed, ill-intentioned films which have made it look as though Arabs belch at the end of a meal. I have heard many stupid things in my lifetime, but nothing so bad as this. If you belch involuntarily and do not beg pardon, you run the risk of someone saying *satteh* to you ('Go to hell' or 'May you explode').
- Give thanks to Allah for the generous gift of such food.
- Before washing their hands, some people suck three fingers (the thumb, index and middle fingers which they have used to eat, thus emulating Muhammad and his co-religionaries. The Prophet justified this with 'No one knows where Allah places the best and the most beneficial part of the meal, in the first mouthful or in the juice that impregnates your fingers.'
- There is nothing better to finish a meal than a glass of cold water.
- After lunch you should have a short nap. When you wake up, have some dessert and then, finally, coffee or tea. However, after dinner, you should go for a walk of at least a hundred paces. There is a well-known Arab proverb that says: *taghada wa tamada, taasha wa tamasha* (Lunch, then a lie-down; dinner, then a walk).

Glossary

Aafuan • عفوان :   Pardon

Ahlan wa Sahlan • أهلا وسهلا :   Welcome

Akleh rajisa • اكل رخيصة :   Cheap menu

Al-hamdu li-llah • الحمد لله :   Thanks be to God

Asef • آسف :   Sorry

As-salam alaíkom • السلام عليكم : Peace be with you and yours

Attchan • عطشان :   To be thirsty

Bajil • بخيل :   Mean

Baraka Allah fik • بارك الله فيك :   May Allah bless you

Bhar • بهار :   Indian spice very similar to curry

Bharat • بهارات :   Mixture of various spices

Bidun sukkar • بدون سكر :   Without sugar

Bismi Allah ar-Rahman ar-Rahim • بسم الله الرحمان الرحيم : In the name of Allah, the Merciful, the Compassionate

Burghul or Bulghur • برغل : Cracked wheat. Can be found in specialist shops or in many supermarkets, often sold under the name of Bulgar wheat

Chabaan • شبعان :   To be satisfied and full of food

Eish • عيش :   Bread (word used in Egypt)

Fulful bhar • فلفل بهار : The special mixture of *bhar* with black or white pepper and some other spice. Buy it ready-made, if you can, from specialist shops, or see p.206 for possible alternatives

Guaan • جوعان :   To be hungry or have an appetite

Hafleh • حفلة :   Feast

Harr • حر :   Hot, peppery

Harisa • هريسة :   In the Maghreb, this means hot or peppery. Harissa paste is available in some of the big supermarkets and in most Arab ones. In the Middle East, however, *harisa* refers to a very popular pastry made with semolina and syrup.

In sha'a Allah • إن شاء الله :   If God so wishes; May…

Jubs or **Jubus** • خبز :   Bread

Judrauat • خضروات :   Greens

Kahua or **qahwa** • قهوة :   Coffee

Kahua saada • قهوة سادة :   Coffee without sugar

Kahua maa halib • قهوة مع حليب :   Coffee with milk

Karch • كرش :   Belly

Karim • كريم :   Splendid, generous, hospitable

Kol • كل :   Eat

Lahm or **Lahmeh** • لحم :   Meat

Laziz • لذيذ :   Delicious

La • لا :   No

Ma'a or **Ma'i** • ماء :   Water

Machrubat or **Mashrubat** • مشروبات :   Drinks

Malh • ملح :   Salt

Marhaba • مرحبا :   Welcome

Masyed or **Dyamea** • مسجد أو جامع :   Mosque

Men fadlak • من فضلك :   Please

Naam or **Tayyeb** (**Waja** واخه in the Maghreb) • نعم أو طيب :   Yes, agreed

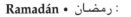

Ramadán • رمضان :   Month of fasting

Sabba bharat • سبع بهارات :   The Lebanese use this mixture of seven different spices, never the same

Samna or **Samneh** • سبع بهارات : Arab clarified butter or ghee

Shatta • شطة :   Hot, peppery (only in Middle East)

Shay • شاي :   Tea

Shukran • شكراً :   Thank you

Shukran li Allah • شكر لله :   Thanks be to God: much used expression

Sukkar • سكر :   Sugar

Summak • سماق :   Dark crimson spice, found in specialist shops

Suq • سوق :   Market, sometimes refers to town centre

Tafaddalu • تفضلوا :   Invitation to enter a house, shop or to join in a meal

Tahanina • تهانينا :   To greet someone

Tahineh or **Tahinah** or **Thinieh** • طحينة :   Sesame sauce or cream

Taman • تمام :   To be satisfied or perfect

Wahed • واحد :   One

Wahed shay • واحد شاي :   One tea

Walimeh or **Aazimeh** • وليمة أو عزيمة   Banquet

Zeyn • زين :   Very good, splendid

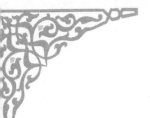

Bibliography

Adab el taam, A. Abdallah. Dar al Aquida Publishers, Alexandria

Adat wa Taqualid end el badu (Customs and Traditions among the Bedouin), Dr el Ueidah, Dar el Bashir Publishers, Amman

Alimentacíon mediterránea (Mediterranean food), Xavier Medina et al., Ed. I.C.M., Barcelona

Alef ba al tabikh (ABC of Cooking), S. Kamal, Dar el elm Publishers, Beirut

Ard al zekrayat (Memorable Earth), Lorteh, Beirut, 1875

Turkish Cooking, I. Cut, Turistik Yayinlar Publishers

Culturas del Magreb, M.A. Roque et al. Ed. I.C.M.

Don Quijote de la Mancha, Cervantes, Biblioteca Hispania

The Koran

Islam, M. Hamildallah, Ed. M de religion. Qatar, 1996

Fisiología del gusto (Physiology of Taste), Brillat-Savarin, I. Juvenil, Barcelona

Folklore, N. Sarhan, Dar al dastur Publishers, Amman

Heraf Arabieh (Arabian Handicrafts), V. Sahab, Al hamra Publishers, Beirut

Qissas al árab (Arab tales), Abu al Fadl, Dar al turaz Publishers, Lebanon, 1963

La cocina del los Califas (Cooking in the time of the Caliphs), L. Benavides, Ed. Dulcinea

La cuisine de Ziryab, F. Mardam, Ed. Sindabad

Le Mezze Libanais (Lebanese Mezze), R. El Kareh, Ed, Sindbad

Marruecos, tierra del sol poniente (Morocco, land of the setting sun), Y. Guardiano, Alianza

Mausuaa Arabieh (Arab Encyclopaedia) A. Saudita and E. Arabes Publishers

Mausuaa Falastinieh (Palestinian Encyclopaedia) Dire Publishers,

Nakha (Aroma), Aziz Shahab, Barhume Publishers, Amman

Refranes y dichos populares comparados (A comparison of popular refrains and sayings) H. Abu-Sharar, Ed. U.A.B., Barcelona, 1998

Recettes de Couscous (Couscous recipes) M. Morsy, Ed. Sindbad

Targhib wa tarhib (Encouragement versus dissuasion), Imam al Muntazery, Dar el hadith Publishers, Cairo

The Arabian Delights, A.M. Weiss Armush, Cookbook Publishers

The Arabs in History, B. Lewis, Edhasa Publishers

Al Turath (Traditions), M. Ali, Farra Publishers, Karmel

Ulumal din (Religious knowledge) U. Khalifeh, Ottoman Publishers, Cairo, 1933

Viaje por Egipto y Asia menor (Journey through Egypt and Asia Minor), R. Mayrat, Ed. Coleccíon

Notes

1 In the Arab world, only two things are exempt from protests about the high volume of their recordings or radiophonic transmissions. These are readings from the Koran, about which no one protests, out of respect, and secondly the voice of the singer Um Kulthum, out of collective delirium.

2 *Storia dei Maccheroni* (History of Macaroni), by Alberto Consiglio (1959), Documents relating to Arab Palermo by Ibn Ghubair.

3 In *Kitaab el tabikh* (The Book of Cooking) both Ibn el Mahdi and el Baghdadi, two great cooks under the Caliphs of that period, mention *maqlouba*.

4 Arabs calls all foreigners with a white skin and blue eyes by this name. The word *faranjas* comes, presumably from the Franks, who participated in the Crusades. It also sounds much like *foreigners*.

5 A legend which is vehemently defended by those living in Hebron, demonstrating that Hebron grapes, as well as being the best, are also divine.

6 When the Arabs of the East talk about the Maghreb, they are referring conjointly to Morocco, Algeria and Tunisia. On the other hand, they say Marrakesh when they're referring to Morocco.

7 In the Middle East they refer to the drug by the names of *mujadarat, hashish* or *afion* but never *kif.*

8 School founded at the beginning of the 1970s in Tlemcen in Algeria, dedicated exclusively to conserving and encouraging the music of Muslim Spain.

[9] The Arabs gives these names, respectively, to the brother of the mother or to some male cousin of the mother. On the other hand, *Ammoh* is the title used when referring to the brother, cousins and friends of the father.

[10] Arab tradition, in which the prospective bride must, as a first act, appear before the family committee of the prospective groom so that they can inspect her.

[11] A pit oven used by the Bedouin, and also once found in villages. It was built in a pit of 2-3 square metres, and covered with a metal dome. The charcoal and wood fuel is positioned along one side. Bedouin bread, in the shape of an enormous pizza, is cooked on the domed lid. It is unique.

[12] Abu Hureira, the great compiler of the *Hadith*, Muhammad's teachings, says that 'the Prophet advised Muslims that they would lose two *Kirat* [a unit of measurement] of divine blessing for each day they made a pet of a dog'. Muhammad only made two exceptions: hunting dogs and shepherd dogs.

[13] United Nations Organisation devoted to helping refugees.

[14] N. Sirhan *Encyclopaedia of Palestinian Folklore*

[15] According to *Lisan el árab* (a treatise on the Arabic language), *mezza* comes from the Arabic verb *tamazzaza* and means to taste in small quantities, a little at a time, thus impregnating the taste buds to achieve maximum enjoyment. *Mezza* is made up of many small dishes that can be nibbled at, and so is rather similar to the appetisers of the West, before the main meal.

[16] It is said that Mejana was the name of a beautiful peasant girl, who was abducted by the headman of a village. Her husband, a poor peasant, resigned to his fate, spent the rest of his life wandering through the mountains and singing heartrending

songs for his beloved. All began with the same melody and the same letters and called out his lover's name, Mejana, Mejana, repeatedly and desperately.

[17] A *rabab* is a kind of primitive violin with only one string, handmade by the Bedouin from goatskin.

[18] Songs from the repertoire of the great Iraqi singer of the 1950s, the late-lamented Nazem el Gazaly.

[19] *Istekbaál* comes from the Arabic verb *istakbala*, which means to receive. The *istekbaál* is an interesting institution, originated, voluntarily, by men in the cities of the Middle East. It is a kind of safety-valve or method of escape, according to whether you're seeing it from a man's or a woman's point of view. Every woman has permission, or the right, to receive her friends into the house, one day a month. There they talk, sing, dance, puff on the traditional *narguilas*, etc. In addition to that, I can assure you that the *istekbaál* is a hotbed of gossip, conspiracy and melodramatic tales of love affairs and hatred among the wives. For my mother, it took place on the first Thursday of every month, and naturally it was one of the worst days of the month for my father. The men were not allowed to enter their own home before the *yayat* – the hens – considered the *isekbaál* to be over (according to the men the women in the *istekbaál* only ever cackled). The man's refusal to enter his own home while the hen-party is in progress stems from an Arab male's horror of being seen publicly involved in female matters; this would presumably reduce his standing in the virility stakes among his fellow men, and also, but more viciously, among those same women.

[20] The vast majority of Arabs rate and recognise tea from its country of origin, ignoring its different grades. In this case I believe my brother-in-law was referring unknowingly to the type of tea the English call breakfast tea.

Notes on Measurements and Spices
for the English Edition

The Spanish 'vaso' has been translated as 'cup' and is equivalent to 200 millilitres (approximately one American cup).

Most of the spices mentioned are available in specialised Arab shops and many ordinary supermarkets. *Fulful bhar* is only one of several popular names for this spice mixture, which also tends to vary slightly from place to place. If you have problems in finding *fulful bhar* in Great Britain, we suggest you use *baharat* (Arabian Mixed Spice) which is available in some Arab shops, and mix this with black or white pepper. If you have difficulty finding *baharat* (Arabian Mixed Spice), you can make your own small jar of it from a mixture of coriander, cumin, cinnamon, cardamom, nutmeg, ginger, bay leaves, pimento, turmeric and cloves. Alternatively you can write to the importer: Afendi Ingredients Ltd, The Mill, 18-22 Chapel Street, Levenshulme, Manchester M19 3QA.

Index of Recipes